# ULTIMATE PUNISHMENT

ALSO BY SCOTT TUROW

*Reversible Errors (2002)*

*Personal Injuries (1999)*

*The Laws of Our Fathers (1996)*

*Pleading Guilty (1993)*

*The Burden of Proof (1990)*

*Presumed Innocent (1987)*

*One L (1977)*

# SCOTT TUROW

# ULTIMATE PUNISHMENT

*A Lawyer's Reflections*

*on Dealing with the*

## DEATH PENALTY

PICADOR

First published 2003 by Farrar, Straus & Giroux, New York

First published in Great Britain 2004 by Picador
an imprint of Pan Macmillan Ltd
Pan Macmillan, 20 New Wharf Road, London N1 9RR
Basingstoke and Oxford
Associated companies throughout the world
www.panmacmillan.com

ISBN 0 330 42688 5 HB

9 8 7 6 5 4 3 2 1

A CIP catalogue record for this book is available from
the British Library.

Printed and bound in Great Britain by
Mackays of Chatham plc, Chatham, Kent

For four friends who have shaped

my life as a lawyer—

*Jeremy Margolis*

*Duane Quaini*

*Thomas P. Sullivan*

*Bill Witkowski*

# CONTENTS

# ULTIMATE PUNISHMENT

# 1

## LAW AND MURDER: MICHELLE THOMPSON AND JEANINE NICARICO

O N FEBRUARY 3, 1984, a young woman named Michelle Thompson and a male friend, Rene Valentine, were forced at gunpoint from the car they'd just entered in a parking lot outide D. Laney's, a nightclub in Gurnee, Illinois, north of Chicago. The gunman walked Valentine a short distance, then shot him in the chest at point-blank range. When the police arrived, Michelle Thompson was gone.

I was an Assistant United States Attorney in Chicago at the time, and my oldest friend in the federal prosecutor's office, Jeremy Margolis, helped direct the FBI's search for Thompson. Initially, the case appeared to be an interstate kidnapping, which is a federal matter. Within a few days, the crime proved to be one within the province of state authorities: murder. Beaten, raped, and strangled, Thompson's body was discovered in Wisconsin. Shortly thereafter,

Hector Reuben Sanchez, an illiterate but ambitious factory worker and burglar, was arrested, along with an accomplice, Warren Peters, Jr., who ultimately agreed to testify against Sanchez.

Deeply enmeshed in the case by now, Jeremy was appointed a special Assistant State's Attorney to help the local prosecutors try Sanchez in state court in Lake County, Illinois. As Jeremy prepared for trial, I spent hours listening to him describe Michelle Thompson's miserable final night. After Sanchez raped Thompson on the floor of the family room in his house, she escaped and dashed, still handcuffed and naked below the waist, through the snow to the back door of a neighbor's, where she pleaded for help. Sanchez found her there and later assuaged the neighbor by telling him that Thompson was drunk and hysterical. The pathos of the neighbor's account of the young woman being led away by Sanchez was heartbreaking. Michelle Thompson had been abused now for several hours, and she offered no further resistance. She was resigned to being tortured and degraded, and hoped only to live—a meager, abased wish that went unfulfilled. Back in his house, Sanchez gagged Michelle Thompson with a strip of cloth, bent her over a washing machine and sodomized her, then strangled her with a nylon strap and a coat hanger. He finished the job by beating her head on the basement floor.

In pursuing the case, the FBI had discovered that nine years earlier Sanchez had murdered his girlfriend, slashing her throat and shooting her, then escaped prosecution by threatening the witnesses. This time Jeremy and the Lake County State's Attorneys were determined that there would be no repetitions. They were seeking the death penalty.

Through Jeremy, I followed the progress of the case

closely. Late in the summer, he and Ray McKoski, then the First Assistant State's Attorney in Lake County, proceeded to trial in Waukegan, Illinois. When Sanchez was convicted and sentenced to death in September 1984, I relished their victory.

That sideline experience remained my only direct exposure to capital prosecutions until 1991, when I was asked to take on the *pro bono* appeal of Alejandro Hernandez. By then I was in private practice as a partner in the Chicago office of Sonnenschein Nath and Rosenthal, a large national firm. I'd known of Hernandez for nearly a decade by now as a co-defendant in what the press commonly referred to as "The Case That Broke Chicago's Heart." On February 25, 1983, Patricia Nicarico, who worked as a school secretary in Naperville, a suburb outside Chicago, had returned home to discover that her front door had been kicked in and that her ten-year-old daughter, Jeanine, was missing. Two days later, the girl's body, blindfolded and otherwise clad only in a nightshirt, was found in a nearby nature preserve. She had died as the result of repeated blows to the head, administered only after she had been sexually assaulted in a number of ways. More than forty law enforcement officers joined a multi-jurisdictional task force organized to hunt down the killer, for whose capture a $10,000 reward was offered.

By early 1984, the case had still not been solved, and a heated primary campaign was under way for the job of State's Attorney in DuPage County. A few days before the primary, on March 6, 1984, Alex Hernandez, Rolando Cruz, and Stephen Buckley were indicted, even though six weeks earlier the State's Attorney had said that there was insufficient evidence to indict anyone.

James Ryan won the election and became the new Du-Page County State's Attorney. (Ryan was elected Attorney General of Illinois in 1994 and served until early 2003, after losing in the November 2002 election, when he was the Republican candidate for Governor.) Ryan's new office took the case against the three defendants to trial in January 1985. The jury deadlocked on Buckley, but Hernandez and Cruz were both convicted and sentenced to death. There was no physical evidence against either of them—no blood, semen, fingerprints, hair, fiber, or other forensic proof. The state's case consisted solely of each man's statements, a contradictory maze of mutual accusations and demonstrable falsehoods as testified to by various informants and police officers. By the time the case reached me, seven years after Hernandez and Cruz were first arrested, the Illinois Supreme Court, in 1988, had reversed the original convictions and ordered separate retrials. Cruz was convicted and sentenced to death again in April 1990. The jury hung in Hernandez's second trial, but the state put him on trial for his life a third time in May 1991. He was found guilty but sentenced to eighty years, rather than to execution.

When Hernandez's trial lawyers, Mike Metnick, Jeff Urdangen, and Jane Raley, approached me, they made a straightforward pitch. Their client was innocent. I didn't believe it. I knew how the system worked. Convict an innocent man once? Not likely, but possible. Twice? Never. And even if it were true, I couldn't envision convincing an appeals court to overturn the conviction a second time. Illinois elects its state court judges, and this was a celebrated child murder.

The lawyers begged me to read the brief that Larry Marshall, a renowned professor of criminal law at Northwestern University, had filed in behalf of Cruz, and to look at the transcripts of Hernandez's trials. By the time I had done this, six weeks later, I knew I had to take the case or stop calling myself a lawyer. Alex Hernandez was innocent.

In June 1985, a few months after Hernandez and Cruz were first convicted, another little girl, Melissa Ackerman, age seven, was abducted and murdered in LaSalle County, about an hour's drive from Jeanine Nicarico's house. Both Melissa and Jeanine were kidnapped in broad daylight, carried away in blankets, sodomized, and murdered in a wooded area. A man named Brian Dugan was arrested for Melissa's murder. In the course of complex plea discussions, his lawyer said that Dugan was prepared to plead guilty not only to the Ackerman killing but to a host of other crimes, including raping and killing two more females. One of the additional women Dugan was prepared to admit he killed was a twenty-seven-year-old nurse named Donna Schnorr. The other was Jeanine Nicarico.

The prosecutors from DuPage County were contacted and invited to question Dugan, through his attorney. The First Assistant, Robert Kilander, and a younger prosecutor met with Dugan's lawyer, but after returning to their office, they refused to accept Dugan's statements or to deal with him further. (Nor did anyone from the DuPage office inform the lawyers for Cruz and Hernandez that another man was prepared to admit to the murder for which their clients were then awaiting execution.)

Faced with DuPage's response, one of the LaSalle County prosecutors contacted the Illinois State Police to be certain that someone looked into the matter. Under the direction of Commander Ed Cisowski, the state police investigated Dugan's admission that he was the lone killer of

Jeanine. By the time they were done, Cisowski had concluded that DuPage had convicted the wrong men. Dugan was not at work at the time of the murder, and a church secretary recalled speaking to Dugan two blocks from the Nicarico home that day. A tire print found where Jeanine's body was deposited matched the tires that had been on Dugan's car. He knew a multitude of details related to the crime that were never publicly revealed, including several facts about the interior of the Nicarico home and the blindfold he'd applied to Jeanine.

Despite all of this, the DuPage County prosecutors attempted, for a decade, to debunk Dugan's confession. Even after Cruz's and Hernandez's second convictions were overturned in July 1994 and in January 1995 as a result of the separate appeals Larry Marshall and I argued, and notwithstanding a series of DNA results that excluded first Hernandez, then Cruz as Jeanine Nicarico's sexual assailant, while pointing directly at Dugan, DuPage continued to pursue the cases. Only after Cruz was acquitted in his third trial, in late 1995, were both men at last freed.

# 2

## A DEATH PENALTY AGNOSTIC

HERNANDEZ AND CRUZ are but two of seventeen men in Illinois who, since the state reestablished capital punishment in 1977, have been sentenced to death and later legally absolved of the murder for which they were convicted. Three men were freed in 1999 alone, the most celebrated of them Anthony Porter, who at one point had been only fifty hours away from execution. Porter was released in February 1999, after Paul Ciolino, a private investigator working with Northwestern University journalism professor David Protess and his students, tracked down a man in Milwaukee who admitted to the crime for which Porter was to die. Following that, in November of the same year, the *Chicago Tribune* published a relentless series about failings in the Illinois capital system, focusing not only on the exonerations and related evidentiary problems but also on the high rate of reversals in Illinois' death cases.

Forty-nine percent of death penalty cases had been reversed for a new trial or a new sentencing, with more than a fifth of those reversals arising because of misconduct by prosecutors. In some reversed cases, defendants had been resentenced to death. But often that was not the case.

The Governor of Illinois, George Ryan (no relation to Jim Ryan), was a Republican who had come into office in January 1999 as a lifelong supporter of the death penalty. While a member of the Illinois legislature, he had voted in favor of reestablishing capital punishment in 1977. Nonetheless, he was dismayed by what confronted him. As of the end of 1999, the overall scorecard was something like this. Since 1977, there had been a few more than 270 persons condemned in Illinois whose cases had progressed through an initial appeal. Twelve had exhausted the seemingly everlasting process that is death penalty litigation and been executed. Thirteen had been exonerated. And about 90, who had their death sentences reversed, received some lesser punishment the next time around. In other words, more than a third of the time Illinois had imposed a capital sentence on persons who either were not guilty, or, on second thought, did not deserve execution.

Given his growing awareness of the system's frequent errors, Governor Ryan found the experience of signing a death warrant for the execution of Andrew Kokoraleis in March 1999 tormenting. Unwilling to repeat that, George Ryan declared a moratorium on further executions on January 31, 2000. Hector Reuben Sanchez, the murderer of Michelle Thompson, was one of roughly 170 prisoners whose death sentence was placed on indefinite hold.

In declaring the moratorium, Governor Ryan labeled Illinois' capital justice system "fraught with error." Six weeks later, he named a fourteen-member "blue-ribbon" Commission to tell him how to reform capital punishment in Illinois. I was one of the persons the Governor appointed to serve.

I had been in the Netherlands on a book tour, driving past flooded farm fields on the way to The Hague, when I was first phoned by Matt Bettenhausen, Illinois' Deputy Governor for Criminal Justice and Public Safety, who became Executive Director of the Commission. I did not hesitate when he asked if I would like to be considered. It was important work and would offer me the chance to systematically contemplate an issue that had long divided me against myself.

I am sure many Illinois residents were startled to see someone whose name they might know as a storyteller chosen to help deliberate about what is probably the gravest real-life problem in the law. Although I spend the majority of my time these days as a writer, I remain a partner in the Chicago office of Sonnenschein. After the publication of my first two novels—*Presumed Innocent* in 1987 and *The Burden of Proof* in 1990—I began to limit my time practicing law, devoting much of it to *pro bono* matters. Thus, in the nineties, the bulk of my hours as lawyer went into the post-trial phases of two very different capital prosecutions, *Hernandez* and a case I took on after that for a young man named Christopher Thomas. These activities did not make me a death penalty expert by any stretch; many of my colleagues on the Commission had dealt with capital cases far more regularly. But I'd had intense personal experiences that certainly gave me a hands-on perspective.

The Governor introduced the Commission at a teeming press conference on March 9, 2000, at the Thompson

Center in Chicago. When one of the reporters asked how many of us opposed capital punishment, only four of the members—former U.S. Senator Paul Simon; Rita Fry and Ted Gottfried, both public defenders; and Bill Martin, who, years ago as a prosecutor, had sent mass-murderer Richard Speck to death row—raised their hands. I had felt no inclination to raise mine.

In college and graduate school, from 1966 to 1972, I adhered to the Aquarian faith of the era. I accepted the fundamental goodness of all people and accordingly regarded capital punishment as barbaric. By 1978, I'd become an Assistant United States Attorney in Chicago. There was no federal death penalty in those years. (It was reenacted in 1988, but only for murders related to a few drug offenses. In 1994, it was expanded to apply to murders in many more circumstances.) That was fine with me when I took the job, and I was somewhat jolted a few months after I'd started, when one of my closest friends in the office, Julian Solotorovsky, was assigned to a murder case. Ralph Perez, a patient at the North Chicago Veterans Administration Hospital, had been watching TV when another patient changed the channel. Ralph responded by stomping the man to death. Under the U.S. criminal code, a state crime committed on federal lands is prosecuted in federal court, but punished according to state law. That meant Ralph was subject to the death penalty.

Julian had been raised a Quaker, and I remember the two of us staring at each other across his desk when we first discussed this prospect. As it happened, Ralph was found incompetent to stand trial, but the fact that seeking capital punishment might conceivably be among my responsibilities was stunning. Could I actually do that?

By 1984, when Jeremy Margolis tried Hector Reuben Sanchez, I'd decided I could. Over my years as a prosecutor, my view of human nature had acquired a far more Hobbesian cast. I'd learned that people who commit crimes are, very often, engaged in an act of self-definition. They do not think much of themselves and they are inclined, as a result, to treat others cruelly. They lie for laughs and do violence, either as a business or because they are angry and it gratifies them. In a normative sense, they are bad people—and they are going to stay that way, in most instances. My job as a prosecutor—and the sensible first response of society—was to make sure they didn't do bad things again. And I could see that a sentence of death was the most certain means to accomplish that goal in extreme cases.

Thus, if I'd had to trade places with Jeremy and ask a jury to condemn Hector Sanchez to death, I believed I could do it. I did not force myself to justify capital punishment, just as I did not routinely question the wisdom of the RICO statute or the mail fraud or securities laws it was my job to enforce. But I could follow the will of my community on the issue.

The ten years I spent in the nineties on the defense side of capital cases taught me many cautionary lessons about the death penalty, but when Matt Bettenhausen called me about serving on the Commission, I still hung in a sort of ethical equilibrium, afraid to come down on either side of the question of whether capital punishment was actually right or wise. Many of the traditional arguments against capital punishment had little traction with me. I respect the religious views of persons who regard life as sacred, but I don't want government action predicated on anybody's religious beliefs. The simple principle that says "If killing is wrong, then the state shouldn't do it" has always struck me as just that—simple, too simple for the complexities of human conduct. Besides, it would also bar certain state violence I accept as a necessity—war or the use of lethal force when called for by police. Nor was I moved by those who denounce the death penalty as revenge, which pretends that getting even isn't one of the motives for putting criminals in prison. How else to explain the stark conditions of American penitentiaries? On the other hand, I had a hard time defining what good came of capital punishment.

When people asked, I referred to myself as a death penalty agnostic. Every time I thought I was prepared to stake out a position, something would drive me back in the other direction. In 1994, while I was representing Hernandez and had seen how wrong capital cases could go, John Wayne Gacy was scheduled for execution. In the late 1970s, Gacy, a contractor and part-time children's-party clown, had raped and murdered approximately thirty-three young men, many of them teenagers, whom he had enticed to his home. According to the accounts of the few survivors, Gacy spent hours practicing tortures straight from Sade on his victims, repeatedly bringing them to the point of death until they finally succumbed, after which Gacy buried their corpses in the crawl space beneath his house. When the death penalty activists, who took me as an ally because of my work on Alex's case, asked me to join their protests of Gacy's execution, I refused. I could not call putting John Wayne Gacy to death an injustice.

By taking a place on the Commission, I knew I would finally have to decide what I would do about capital punishment if I were, in the favorite law school phrase, "czar of the universe." Paul Simon, the former U.S. Senator who was one of our co-chairs and a longtime foe of the death penalty, served notice at the threshold that before our labors were completed, he intended to call the question of whether Illinois should have capital punishment. As a lawyer, I was accustomed to working on matters one case at a time. Now I would have to pass judgment on an entire system, cast a vote, and give the people of Illinois my best advice, for whatever it was worth. No more dodging my conscience, no more mouthing liberal pieties while secretly hoping some conservative showed up to talk hard-nosed realities. The omen of that day of decision would, for me, loom over the whole enterprise. I was going to have to decide.

# 3
—

## GOVERNOR GEORGE RYAN

THE MAN who declared Illinois' moratorium on executions and who appointed me to his Commission on Capital Punishment remains one of the more enigmatic figures in recent local history. On looks, George Ryan, snow-capped and agreeably round, might be mistaken for an applicant for a seasonal opening as a department store Santa, but his tenure as Illinois' Governor from January 1999 to January 2003 was not always jolly. Throughout his years in the Executive Mansion, Ryan was engulfed by a scandal focused on the office he held before being elected Governor, when he was Illinois' Secretary of State. By the time Ryan left office, at least fifty persons, many Ryan's former Secretary of State employees, had been convicted in federal court, most of them in connection with selling drivers' licenses for bribes. Worse, both Ryan's ex-chief of staff and Ryan's political campaign fund had been indicted (and were later convicted in March 2003) for racketeering in connection with an alleged scheme to defraud taxpayers by using the workers and facilities of the Secretary of State's office for Ryan's gubernatorial campaign. Rumors of the Governor's imminent indictment were rife during much of his time in office.

Despite this, Ryan neither circled the wagons nor ducked tough issues that risked further eroding his political support. A moderate-to-conservative Republican, Ryan had nonetheless run to the left of his pro-gun, anti-abortion Democratic opponent during the election. Whatever the hopes of conservative Republicans, in office Ryan hewed to the moderate agenda he promised, which was very much in line with the middle-of-the-road approach that had kept Republican governors in power in Illinois for decades. He aided business interests, but instead of a tax cut, he used the budget surplus he found when he entered office in 1999 to reverse the prevailing trend of starving schools and roads. He visited Cuba in hopes of selling Illinois agricultural products, vetoed a bill to cut off Medicaid funding of abortions, and supported anti-gun legislation.

Professionally, Ryan was a pharmacist who'd run a chain of family-owned drugstores in Kankakee, a small Illinois city just far enough from Chicago to be outside the bright lights. He started in politics in the 1960s on the county board, eventually becoming Illinois' Speaker of the House from 1981 to 1983. He served two four-year terms as Lieutenant Governor, then spent eight years as Secretary of State, before finally being elected Governor in 1998, culminating what surely must have been a lifelong dream. He is the image of the plain-spoken, unworldly Midwesterner, pragmatic and determinedly unimpressed with himself. At a dinner in the home of a mutual friend, I watched Governor Ryan get up from the table to clear his own plate; guests who spent the night at the Executive Mansion reported that before going to bed, the Governor walked around turning off the lights.

When he spoke privately about some of his tougher decisions as Governor, including the death penalty issue, Ryan often referred to his experience as a pharmacist. I think he saw his role in government as not all that different—he was trying to help people overcome what ailed them. The sheer harshness of the death penalty always seemed to me inconsistent with the core of George Ryan's character.

That said, Illinois politics is a rough-and-tumble world and one with a long tradition of public officials who somehow find their hands—or those of their friends—in the cookie jar. The corruption allegations that swirled throughout Ryan's term were not the first lodged against him. Speculation about the Governor's motives in championing a cause as unpopular as death penalty reform was a favorite parlor game. Was he trying to deflect attention from the grand jury probe? Was he hoping to create another legacy besides scandal?

I had never met George Ryan when he was elected, although, like many other nominal Democrats, I had supported him as the better choice on the issues when he ran for Governor. Not long after Ryan's election, I spent two days at a state literary event where the Governor-elect's wife, Lura Lynn, was representing her husband, who as Secretary of State was also Illinois' official Librarian. Mrs. Ryan is a charmer—good-humored, straightforward, and bright. She spoke candidly about political life, and one of the things she told me was that her husband, who would be sixty-eight at the end of his term, had promised her he would not run for reelection. Mrs. Ryan was far too experienced in politics to take that at face value and said as much. But in the years that ensued, as others castigated George Ryan and looked askance at his motives, I remembered what Mrs. Ryan had said. To me, George Ryan always appeared to be somebody who knew the rehearsal was over. In the time he had, on the issues that counted, he was simply going to do what was right.

# 4

## AMERICA AND THE DEATH PENALTY

WHATEVER George Ryan's character or motives, there can be no dispute that Ryan's decision to declare the moratorium was the first act in a national reassessment of the death penalty that is quite clearly under way. In May 2002, Parris Glendenning, the Governor of Maryland, followed Ryan's example and suspended executions in his state for a year, pending a study of racial disparities in who gets sentenced to death. (The report by Raymond Paternoster of the University of Maryland was released on January 7, 2003, and concluded that both race and geography affect death penalty decisions in Maryland, but the new Governor, Robert Ehrlich, has vowed to lift the moratorium, a position that probably gained appeal in the wake of the Beltway Sniper killings.) The state of Indiana established a Criminal Law Study Commission in 2001 to look at various issues related to the death penalty. In March of 2003, a committee appointed by the Pennsylvania Supreme Court recommended halting all executions in the state until the reasons for apparent racial bias in the application of the death penalty in the state are better understood.

The American judiciary also seems to be exhibiting a new willingness to restrict the death penalty, led by the U.S. Supreme Court. In June 2002, the Court ruled that a defendant who has elected a jury trial has a constitutional right to have that jury, rather than a judge, decide if he will be sentenced to death. The ruling brought into question death sentences imposed in nine different states. Furthermore, based on that holding, in September a federal judge in Vermont said the federal capital punishment statute is unconstitutional because it lacks adequate safeguards on the evidence presented to juries to obtain a death verdict.

Even more significantly, perhaps, the Supreme Court also ruled in 2002 that execution of the mentally retarded is unconstitutional as cruel and unusual punishment. The decision invites extended litigation about how capable a human being must be before execution is constitutionally acceptable. At the start of the Supreme Court's next term, in October 2002, four justices expressed the view that executing murderers who were under eighteen at the time of their crime is also cruel and unusual punishment. Their consensus essentially guarantees that the entire Court will eventually decide this question (which may well determine the fate of Lee Malvo, who is facing a capital trial in Virginia for the Beltway Sniper shootings he allegedly committed at age seventeen).

The Supreme Court's new latitude toward death penalty issues continued in its next term. In 2003, the Court nudged the door wider for post-conviction review in federal court for capital cases and raised the bar for a defense lawyer's duty to seek out mitigating evidence for a capital sentencing hearing.

This, of course, is not the first time that America and its courts have thought twice about the wisdom of killing killers. One need only glance at a TV screen to realize that murder remains a national preoccupation, and the concomitant questions of how to deal with it have long challenged contending strains in American moral thought, pitting Old Testament against New, retribution against forgiveness.

To some extent, the debate about capital punishment has been going on almost since the founding of the Republic. At that time, each state, following the English tradition, imposed death for a long list of felonies. But the same humanism that posited the equal value of all men and animated democracy necessarily led to many questions about a punishment that vested such fierce power over citizens in the state and assumed individuals were irredeemable. Jefferson was among the earliest advocates of restricting executions, and in 1794, Pennsylvania limited capital punishment to first-degree murder. In 1846, Michigan became the first American state to outlaw capital punishment for killers.

Public support for capital punishment has waxed and waned in the United States throughout our history. In 1966, opinion polls showed for the first time that a majority of Americans opposed capital punishment. Inspired, perhaps, by the seeming evolution in prevailing standards, the U.S. Supreme Court in 1972 held in *Furman v. Georgia* that in the three cases before the Court, the death penalty constituted cruel and unusual punishment, with the justices in the majority noting the utter caprice with which American juries were allowed to decide whether a defendant lived or died. But the turmoil of the sixties had led to a new American passion for law and order, and the *Furman* decision inspired a powerful political backlash. Several states passed new death penalty laws, and in 1976 the Court decided that Georgia's revised and more exacting capital statute, designed to more closely confine a jury's discretion in imposing death, was constitutional after all. Two justices, Byron R. White and Potter Stewart, who had found the death penalty cruel and unusual in *Furman*, approved the Georgia statute, as did Justice John Paul Stevens, who had replaced William O. Douglas in the interval. Illinois, along with many other states, quickly followed suit with a new capital law patterned after Georgia's.

But in the 1990s, the advent of DNA testing repeatedly showed that innocent people had been convicted of violent crimes. Many of the exonerated were on death row. As of May 2003, the Death Penalty Information Center counted 108 persons who have been sentenced to death in the United States and later legally absolved. And there are dozens of additional cases that fall short of outright exoneration where emerging questions have led the condemned to be freed. The prospect of error seems to be the leading cause in reduced support for the death penalty. In the most recent polling, early in 2003, a plurality of only 49 percent of Americans favored capital punishment, when offered the alternative of life in prison without parole.

For most Americans, the death penalty debate goes no further than asking whether they "believe" in capital punishment. There is good reason for this, of course, because the threshold issues define us so profoundly as individuals and as a society that it is almost impossible to move past them. What are the goals of punishment? What do we think about the perfectibility of human beings and the perdurability of evil? What value do we place on life—of the murderer and of the victim? What kind of power do we want in the hands of government, and what do we hope the state can accomplish when it wields it?

One of the reasons that the death penalty debate so preoccupies us is because of the essential nature of these questions. Almost no one feels detached about capital punishment. Advocates, opponents, and those in conflict all see in the issue a struggle for the national soul. Many death penalty opponents who root their position in religious or spiritual convictions treat those who favor death sentences as barbarians or wanton sinners. Supporters of capital punishment frequently characterize those on the other side as bleeding hearts and hypocrites, who would never feel the same way were it their loved ones who had been murdered. These volleys of mutual accusation have often drowned out the nuances in the national debate and, I suspect, masked the degree to which large numbers of Americans, like me, have long approached these questions with some residue of doubt. The truth, I suspect, is that as crimes and cases unfold around us, many of us often feel a visceral attraction to both positions.

# 5

## THE COMMISSION

GOVERNOR RYAN'S COMMISSION on Capital Punishment was clearly assembled to represent diverse viewpoints and experience. Among the fourteen of us, there were prominent Democrats and Republicans, three women, and four members of minority groups. Twelve were attorneys, including a former Chief Judge of the federal district court, two sitting State's Attorneys, two public defenders, and a number of lawyers who'd walked on both sides. Over the years, eleven of us had been prosecutors, while nine of us had experience as defense lawyers. And Paul Simon, a journalist by training, had helped write the laws as a United States Senator.

The criminal bar, even in a large city, resembles a small town, and I had shared stretches in my lawyering life, often very large and significant ones, with many of my colleagues. One of the Commission co-chairs, Tom Sullivan, long a partner at a prominent Chicago firm, had been the United States Attorney who hired me fresh out of Harvard Law School and who, in time, became my principal mentor as an attorney. Andrea Zopp, now General Counsel of Sears, had been, by turns, a young lawyer I'd helped train in the U.S. Attorney's Office, then, years later, the First Assistant State's Attorney for Cook County, which encompasses Chicago, and after that, my law partner. Our chair, Frank McGarr, was a former federal judge, before whom I had tried a number of cases. The Executive Director, Matt Bettenhausen, had the same pedigree as a lawyer that I did—Sonnenschein and the U.S. Attorney's Office, albeit in reverse order—and thus we'd been crossing paths for more than a decade. I knew Mike Waller, the State's Attorney in Lake County, the third most populous county in Illinois, because I dealt with him for years in the course of representing Christopher Thomas, a young man whom Mike's office had sent to death row. My *pro bono* work had put me in frequent contact with Rita Fry, the Public Defender of Cook County, and with Ted Gottfried, the State Appellate Defender for Illinois. And I couldn't count the number of cases I'd had with Bill Martin, literally a lawyers' lawyer, an ethics expert who, after his time as a prosecutor, often represented attorneys facing professional discipline. I'd also interacted often with Don Hubert when he'd been president of the Chicago Bar Association.

Naturally, I didn't know everybody the Governor appointed. Kathy Dobrinic was from downstate Montgomery County, now finishing her third term as State's Attorney there. She was president-elect of the state association of county prosecutors. Tom Needham, another former Assistant State's Attorney in Cook County, was the chief of staff to the superintendent of the Chicago Police Department. Perhaps the Governor's most intriguing appointment was Roberto Ramirez; he and former Senator Simon were the lone Commission members without law degrees. A Mexican American immigrant who'd built a successful janitorial business, Roberto knew more than he wanted about violent death. His father had been murdered, and his grandfather had shot and killed the man who was responsible.

With the exception of Roberto, we were all bound up in the same network of long-term relationships that gave us a solid footing to start. But very often these kinds of bodies accomplish little. Members are polite to one another, very pleased with themselves for sharing such esteemed company, and much too busy doing the stuff that made them eligible for membership in the first place to make much of an effort. Our group was different. The assignment was different. And all of us, Republicans and Democrats, were probably inspired because George Ryan had taken such large risks in declaring the moratorium. We all accepted the Governor's premise that Illinois' capital punishment system required scrutiny. And we all came with an appreciation for the profound complexities of capital punishment as a legal, political, and moral issue. We arrived with our experiences and our opinions, but from the start, there was virtually no posing. Nobody ever pretended that he or she couldn't understand the contrary point of view or, in fact, had not been reached by many of its claims.

The essential question the Governor posed to the Commission was this: What reforms, if any, would make application of the death penalty in Illinois fair, just, and accurate? Everyone on the Commission agreed that the inquiry by its nature required that we first consider reforms before we could ask whether the resulting system met the various tests of fairness. Our foremost task was pragmatic: identify problems and propose solutions. The big issues would come at the end.

One of the initial assignments the Governor had given us was to study in depth the cases of those who had been sentenced to death in Illinois and later exonerated. Looking at these cases together—there were thirteen at that time—we had to determine if there were endemic problems that could be isolated and remedied.

We spent a number of months doing this. Many of our findings flew in the face of what I had taken for granted during my years as a prosecutor, and even as a defense lawyer. For instance, one of the fixed stars of the universe of criminal justice is the idea that nobody voluntarily confesses to a crime she or he didn't commit. For this reason, a confession is regarded as the best possible evidence, and cops work hard in their interrogations of suspects to get admissions to the crime. Informed estimates are that confessions are obtained in roughly 40 percent of arrests, and that in nearly a quarter of all prosecuted cases the defendant would not be convicted but for his own incriminating statements.

Thus, the persistence of purported confessions by innocent people in Illinois' exonerated cases was a wake-up call to me, albeit one where I'd heard the first ring years before. The only evidence that Alex Hernandez had any actual role in the murder of Jeanine Nicarico was a declaration he supposedly made to a state informant: "All I did was hold that little girl down, while they hit her in the head." The alleged statement was shocking—but so were the circumstances under which it was said to have been gathered.

Alex's IQ was low—defense experts put it at 73—and psychologists for both sides testified that his behavior years ago reflected what a sense of his deficits could produce in a young person: a tendency to seek attention, especially by telling wild tales. Alex had come forward originally in response to public reports of the $10,000 reward, claiming to know something about a mysterious Ricky who'd spoken of the murder, but Alex's so-called information only led the police in circles. Well aware of Alex's problems, the police continued to assure Alex he would be rewarded for helping them, even though they regarded him as a suspect (notwithstanding the fact that he had only a single misdemeanor conviction for theft).

One day, they put Alex in a room with a childhood friend, Armindo Marquez, who was in custody on a burglary rap. The police had instructed Marquez to say—falsely—that he had information about another murder in Bolingbrook, a nearby town, and to suggest that Alex and he tell police details of that case and the Nicarico murder and then share the $10,000 reward. To cement the idea, detectives actually put a shoe box filled with cash in the room and had Marquez tell Alex it was the reward money. Marquez never required that what Alex and he tell the cops be true, and the record shows instead that they were making it up as they went along. Marquez spun out a bunch of phony details of the Bolingbrook crime, and Alex, who thought he was there to aid police and had been told that he could get the reward by extracting the Bolingbrook information, responded with a number of statements about the Nicarico murder. It was in this context that Alex supposedly said, "I held her down." Virtually every other statement he made about the crime that was capable of extrinsic verification proved to be false. To make it worse, after he was out of jail, Marquez said that his testimony against Alex was fabricated. Nor did the state ever explain how someone, no matter how weak-minded, would believe he could confess to a horrible murder and be free to use reward money. Logic notwithstanding, though, Alex spent the next twelve years in the penitentiary.

Interrogation techniques that clearly risked eliciting false statements were not limited to Hernandez's case. Gary Gauger was the first to discover the body of his father in April 1993, in the family motorcycle shop in McHenry County, an exurban area west of Chicago. When the police arrived, they found Gauger's mother slain as well, and took Gauger as the prime suspect in the murders. They interrogated him for twelve hours, until he made a statement which the police called a confession, and which Gauger says was a hypothetical discussion they encouraged about how the murder occurred. Gauger—whose case is among those depicted in the popular play *The Exonerated*—was sentenced to death. Years later, two members of the Outlaws motorcycle gang were convicted of crimes that included the Gauger parents' murders.

Sometimes the methods utilized in gaining statements were not subtle. Ronald Jones, convicted of a rape and murder in Chicago in 1985, maintained that his confession had been beaten out of him. The state claimed the marks visible on Jones's face at the time he was arrested were from a skin condition. Years later, DNA evidence categorically established that Jones's confession was false.

And there was also the Cruz case, where a grand jury found probable cause to believe there was no confession at all. The police claimed Cruz had told them about a vision of the crime, filled with details only the killer could know. Yet somehow the DuPage officers also maintained they had forgotten about the statement until days before the start of Rolando's and Alex's trial in 1985 and had also neglected to make any written report of it in the first place—remarkable lapses given usually rigid law enforcement practices.

While false confessions were the dominating problem in the Illinois exonerations, and have appeared in other jurisdictions, as in New York City's Central Park jogger case, where DNA evidence indicated five young men had gone to the penitentiary for a rape committed by someone else, the thirteen Illinois cases also called into question other forms of evidence in which courts and lawyers have long placed confidence. When I started trial practice twenty-five years ago, an eyewitness was regarded as the evidentiary gold standard. What better proof could you have than a bystander who saw the whole crime take place and could thus confidently name the perpetrator? Subsequent psychological research has demonstrated that the sheer extraordinariness of witnessing a crime challenges perception. Anthony Porter was falsely identified as a multiple killer by two people who had often seen him around the neighborhood where they all lived. Stephen Buckley, Cruz and Hernandez's original co-defendant, who bears some resemblance to Brian Dugan, was also identified as having been near the crime scene by an eyewitness. Indeed, mistaken identification has been named as the leading cause of wrongful convictions nationwide.

On the other hand, sometimes the road to death row in

these cases had led along byways long recognized as dangerous to the truth. The risk that accomplices and jailhouse snitches will lie to win leniency in their own cases is traditionally acknowledged in jury instructions, which tell jurors, for example, that the testimony of such persons "must be considered with caution and great care." Joseph Burrows, Verneal Jimerson, and Dennis Williams were all sent to death row by the bogus inventions of co-defendants.

Whatever the particulars of these cases, though, the bottom line was the same. Being accused of a grisly murder was a far greater peril to an innocent person than I'd recognized years before.

# 6

## CONVICTING THE INNOCENT

UNDERLYING THE EXONERATIONS in Illinois' death row cases were a few fundamental questions. How could experienced police officers and prosecutors be taken in by false evidence—or even assume a role in manufacturing it? And how could juries fail in their enshrined role of protecting against such abuses and actually buy in?

Thinking about Alex's case and studying the other exonerations in Illinois, I eventually recognized that there is a unique array of factors in death penalty cases that can lead to wrongful convictions. Prosecutors in capital cases have extraordinary leverage over the accused. Defendants who avoid the death penalty do so most often by pleading guilty. Inherent in capital punishment is the risk that an innocent person faced with the choice of living or dying might plead. Many others, of course, accept the peril and demand a trial. When they get it, the law requires removing from the jury any person who says he or she will refuse to impose a capital sentence. It is difficult to imagine what else the law might do other than banish those who will not adhere to its command, but studies have repeatedly asserted that the resulting jury pool is more conviction-prone.

Yet at the end of the day, the factor that is the greatest snare for the innocent is the nature of the cases themselves. In Illinois, in the last twenty-five years, approximately one in every fifty convictions for first-degree murder has resulted in a capital sentence. Even in Wyoming, which has the highest death-sentencing rate in the country, fewer than 6 percent of homicides end up with a sentence of execution pronounced. That is consistent with the command of the U.S. Supreme Court, which has ruled that death may not be the automatic punishment for first-degree murder. In practice, capital punishment is reserved for "the worst of the worst," that is, those crimes which most outrage the conscience of the community. Paradoxically, this makes for the capital system's undoing, because it is these extreme and repellent crimes that provoke the highest emotions—anger, especially, even outrage—that in turn make rational deliberation problematic for investigators, prosecutors, judges, and juries.

Under enormous pressure to solve these cases, police often become prisoners of their own initial hunches. A homicide investigation is not an academic inquiry allowing for even-handed consideration of every hypothesis. Instead, it's conducted in an atmosphere where primitive fears about unknown, dangerous strangers imperil our sense of an orderly world. There is a strong emotional momentum to adopt any explanation. Cops often feel impelled to take the best lead and run with it.

A few weeks before Jeanine's murder, the Nicaricos had hired a Spanish-surnamed cleaning lady who turned out to have a son with a burglary record. He ultimately proved to be blameless in this case, but from that start grew the police theory that the crime had been intended to be a burglary, committed by a gang of Hispanics—even though no valuables were ever found missing from the Nicarico house. When Alex appeared, telling tales, he fit an existing preconception, a theory to which many officers became wedded the longer it persisted, making it virtually impossible for them to accept the fact that a white serial rapist, namely, Brian Dugan, was the actual culprit.

If law enforcement professionals respond in this fashion to the emotionalism of grave crimes, it is foolhardy to expect anything better from the lay people who sit on juries. By the time of Alex's third trial, in May 1991, the evidence against him was so scant that the DuPage County State's Attorney's Office actually sought an outside legal opinion to determine whether they had enough proof to get the case over the bare legal threshold required to ask a jury to decide the matter. By then, Dugan had admitted to the crime and DNA had excluded Alex as the rapist. John Sam, one of the lead detectives on the case, had quit the force because he believed DuPage had accused the wrong men, a point of view shared by the chief of police in Naperville, James Teal. And Marquez, who'd reported the I-held-her-down statement, had now disavowed his testimony.

Instead, the state tried to offer the Marquez evidence

through a police officer who'd been outside the room where Marquez and Hernandez met. The officer testified that he had no memory at all of the conversation. All he could do was recite the contents of a report he'd put together three weeks after the event, long after Marquez's version of the encounter was known. The officer couldn't understand Spanish, in which he acknowledged most of the conversation was conducted. He admitted being twelve feet from the door to the room and even at that didn't know whether it was open or closed. He conceded that he'd destroyed his notes and that what he'd written down at the time wasn't verbatim. And he had no memory of a single word Marquez had spoken to prompt the fragmentary responses from Alex contained in the police report. Later, the trial judge, John Nelligan, remarked, "It is impossible to determine the context . . . not to mention the obvious meaning of the language [the officer] recorded."

But even though a veteran trial judge couldn't place any meaning on what he referred to as "the one statement that tied this Defendant indirectly to involvement in the death of Jeanine Nicarico," the jury convicted. The case demonstrated to me the propensity of juries to turn the burden of proof against defendants accused of monstrous crimes. The notion of a ten-year-old girl being overpowered by an intruder and dragged from the safety of her parents' home, sexually tortured, and then in the end beaten to death is so revolting that I used to explain Alex's and Rolando's convictions by saying that I thought Mother Teresa might have been in jeopardy if she were in the defendant's seat. Jurors are unwilling to take the chance of releasing a monster into our midst, and thus will not always require proof beyond a reasonable doubt.

An enduring problem is that the standards for review of juries' fact-finding decisions in these highly emotional cases is the same as when a defendant is accused of stealing candy from a five-and-dime. Appellate courts are asked to assess whether *any* rational jury could have reached this conclusion, with the italics in place when the legal standard is stated. In so doing, courts must take all evidence "in the light most favorable to the verdict," meaning that they must draw all inferences from the evidence and resolve all credibility questions in a way that supports the jury's decision. An appellate judge's own nagging doubts about an unsavory state witness or the unlikeliness of the prosecutor's theory about motive may not lead to setting the verdict aside. In Alex's case, this meant that even though Judge Nelligan personally regarded the meaning of Alex's exchanges with Marquez as "impossible to determine," he was not empowered to overturn the jury's verdict; the best he could do was refuse to impose a death sentence and give Alex eighty years. When my colleagues, Matt Tanner and Leslie Suson, and I appeared before the Illinois Appellate Court and I argued Alex's appeal, I found the judges similarly skeptical of the same evidence, and I believe their observations from the bench ultimately led the prosecutors to decide not to re-prosecute. But even though the court reversed the judgment, given the deference to a jury's findings, the justices, like Judge Nelligan, could not say that the verdict was completely irrational, which is what the law requires for an outright acquittal on appeal.

Aside from reviewing a verdict once to ensure it's within the broad borders of rationality, the courts by rule are precluded from ever dealing much with the facts of a case again. Although many Americans complain about the parade of years that goes into death penalty litigation, the proceedings after trial never again directly involve the question of whether the defendant is actually guilty. Instead, they usually center on repeated assaults on the competence of the trial lawyers, because that, generally speaking, is the only avenue for attack that is open. But the appellate courts refuse to allow a defendant to, in the parlance, "retry his case." Guilt is taken as a fact determined, even when a defendant has marshaled substantial new evidence that the jury never heard.

Years before he was released, Anthony Porter's lawyers had developed a good deal of proof that Alstory Simon, not Porter, had committed the murders for which Porter sat on death row. Five different times, the Illinois and federal courts refused even to grant Porter an evidentiary hearing, because of the supposed strength of the original trial evidence and because of various rules limiting those courts' rights to reweigh it.

There are reasons for the law's reluctance to allow appellate courts to reconsider the evidence. It would reduce the traditional power of the jury, a citizen bulwark against abuses by the state, if appeals courts could just ignore a jury's conclusions. Besides, appeals court judges haven't seen the witnesses testify, haven't had the opportunity to assess demeanor or to absorb the thousands of details that we take in when we encounter one another in person. And trials would be unending if defendants could keep coming up with one more scrap of information to establish their innocence after verdicts had been entered.

Yet in the charged atmosphere of capital cases, which so tempt juries to allow emotion to guide their decisions, some limited means of verifying the jury's findings ought to be in place, at least if we want to continue to impose the death penalty. And given the propensities of juries in these cases, when a condemned prisoner claims he has mustered new evidence of his innocence, courts must be more open to an unbiased evaluation of that proof.

It goes without saying that even those who support capital punishment recoil at the prospect of executing the innocent. For most of us there is a special horror in this that is difficult even to fully articulate. It's not as if imprisoning an innocent person for life is anything other than a horrific abuse of human rights; but an unwarranted execution is measurably worse. As the courts often succinctly put it, "Death is different." Part of it is the fact that as long as a prisoner lives, there's some hope he can establish his innocence. (In fact, four of the persons on America's death rows at the time *Furman* saved them were ultimately exonerated.) More of our revulsion, I think, stems from the fact that executing the innocent stands justice on its head, making the law a force of barbarism rather than of civilization.

Some of the bravest advocates of capital punishment have been willing to acknowledge that having a capital system will inevitably entail executing someone who is innocent. They argue that what we gain with the death penalty is worth the cost—and point to other social conventions, such as the use of the automobile or alcohol or childhood inoculations, which we tolerate despite knowing that innocent lives will be lost.

But when it comes to an institution as idealized as justice, I doubt most Americans are comfortable with the trade. For the majority of us, the prospect of executing someone who is blameless casts a special pall over the death penalty. The fact that capital cases are uniquely prone to error calls either for safeguards we have yet to institutionalize—or even fully conceive of—or for renewed reflection about whether to proceed with capital punishment at all.

# 7

## BAD FAITH

SHOULD A DEMOCRATIC STATE ever be permitted to kill its citizens? The question may sound like PoliSci 101, but it has an essential place in discussion of the death penalty. If the people are the ultimate source of authority in a democracy, should the government be allowed to eliminate its citizens, who are supposed to be a superior power? As a lawyer who tended to see the death penalty debate in the constitutional terms in which it has been presented—as an unduly cruel punishment, or a maddeningly arbitrary one—I had attended less to the relevant issues of political theory until I visited the American Academy in Berlin in 2000 and discussed capital punishment in the United States. After my address, a law professor, perhaps as old as ninety, rose with obvious difficulty and said, "Here, vee could neffer efen consider again allowing zee state to kill."

His implicit reference to Germany's Nazi past contained not only a sobering reminder of the lessons of history but a powerful and elegant argument. If the government is never permitted to end the life of its citizens, then any such killing would mark an outlaw regime.

I am one of those who tend to find Western European criticisms of capital punishment somewhat misplaced, because Europeans generally overlook how different their circumstances are from ours. The murder rate in the United States is about four times that in the European Union. It is probably not fair that Europeans judge us without living in a society as divided as ours, as fractious and dangerous, a society where the fear, grief, and outrage that murder inspire are far more prevalent.

As important, the American and European pasts offer different omens. Despite Western Europeans' frequent self-congratulation on their civility, it is, in fact, their democracies that have repeatedly been overwhelmed by dictators. Franco. Mussolini. Salazar. Hitler. Pétain. Where democracy has proven fragile, the day seems far less remote when another madman can commandeer the power of the state to kill his enemies. In the U.S., we have, in the last five years alone, endured impeachment of our President, a controverted election of his successor, and a devastating attack on American soil by a foreign force. Despite these disruptions, we have never once seen troops in our streets to restrain citizens. I have always felt that it tempts fate too much to say, as Sinclair Lewis would have it, "It can't happen here," but we must bear in mind that American opinion about capital punishment is subtly dependent on the extraordinary stability of our democratic institutions.

This doesn't mean, however, that the problem of bad faith by governmental officials has no place in discussion of the death penalty. In Illinois, we have 102 elected State's Attorneys, each with the power of life and death in his or her hands while confronting a frightened electorate demanding quick justice, as the public inevitably does in the face of ghastly murders. It is not simple posturing to say that most prosecutors withstand these pressures with professionalism. But even if only a few in a hundred proceed with a blind eye to the facts or the law, the results are unacceptable.

To sidestep the powerful evidence of Brian Dugan's guilt, the state, in Alex Hernandez's second trial, tried to suggest that Alex could have been there with Dugan, notwithstanding the lack of any evidence the men so much as knew each other (or any explanation why one of them wouldn't have named the other to save his life). Nonetheless, to prove there was more than one intruder at the Nicarico home, the prosecutors emphasized two different shoeprints that had been found behind the house, near a window where would-be burglars, supposedly including Alex, could have looked inside. The shoeprints were mentioned in the prosecutor's opening statement, and nine prosecution witnesses were questioned about them, attempting to establish that the prints were connected to Jeanine's disappearance. One of the witnesses testified that Alex, who stands five foot three, admitted to the grand jury that he wore size-seven shoes. Then a shoeprint expert testified that the prints in question were "about a size six."

On cross-examination, the defense lawyer, Mike Metnick, probing this testimony, eventually asked:

Q: And when you say six, are you referring to a male's size six?

A: That would be a female's size six.

Indeed, not only had the expert employed the far smaller woman's size in his testimony about the shoe prints but it also turned out that the tread pattern on one print had been identified as made by a shoe manufactured for women. The expert had known this for a week and had told the prosecutor, Robert Kilander, the First Assistant State's Attorney, before getting on the stand. Kilander never informed the defense lawyers that the print came from a woman's shoe, and simply offered the expert's testimony against Alex Hernandez, a male—and a man on trial for his life.

When Metnick, Urdangen, and Raley moved for a mistrial, Kilander claimed, "I had no knowledge there was any difference between a female and male size six shoe." That still didn't go to explain why he withheld the fact that one print could be proven to be from a woman's shoe. He answered that in a separate hearing several months later. "It slipped my mind," Kilander said.

Defense lawyers lob empty accusations of misconduct at prosecutors and cops all the time. But in the Nicarico prosecutions, judges agreed. The first joint trial of Hernandez and Cruz was reversed by the Illinois Supreme Court because of what it labeled "a deliberate and constitutionally unacceptable attempt by the prosecution" to convict each man with evidence inadmissible against him. Despite that, the improperly motivated injection of more inadmissible proof was one of the grounds for reversal when the Illinois Supreme Court set aside Cruz's second conviction. In that opinion and in the first Hernandez reversal, the Supreme Court also commented on two instances in which DuPage had allowed jailhouse witnesses to testify they had no deal with the prosecutors; the Court noted that on each occasion the trial prosecutors in fact had spoken up for each man when he was sentenced.

In 1995, following the second reversal of Cruz's conviction and death sentence, he chose to be tried by a judge alone, since Rolando's lawyers had come to accept that a jury would never see this case for what it was. However, the third Cruz trial came to an abrupt end when a police officer, who'd earlier corroborated two colleagues' account of Cruz's "vision statement," now returned to court to acknowledge that his prior testimony was false. The officer said he'd discovered he'd actually been in Florida at the time the other cops had supposedly recounted the vision statement to him.

Judge Ronald Mehling acquitted Rolando, and a few months later the case against Alex was dismissed. In the ensuing uproar, a special grand jury was convened, resulting in the indictment of seven men—three former prosecutors and four members of the DuPage County Sheriff's police—on various charges, including conspiring to obstruct justice in the Cruz case. They were tried and, as is often the case when law enforcement officers are charged with overzealous execution of their duties, acquitted, although the county subsequently reached a multimillion-dollar settlement in civil suits brought by Hernandez, Cruz, and their one-time co-defendant, Stephen Buckley.

Accepting that jury's verdict that none of the seven men acted with criminal intent, I still marvel how little chastening there has been in DuPage County. Joe Birkett, Jim

Ryan's eventual successor as State's Attorney, celebrated at the victory party for his indicted colleagues the night of their acquittal. He recently admitted that DNA establishes Dugan's role with "scientific certainty," but still refuses to acknowledge Cruz and Hernandez's innocence.

On the other hand, the judges in the criminal division attempted to strip Ronald Mehling of his position as Presiding Judge, after he acquitted Cruz. While that effort failed in the face of a public outcry, Mehling decided to resign in 2002. When he did, he had to pay for his own retirement party. In the meantime, Robert Kilander, the prosecutor who tried to send Alex Hernandez to death with the print from a woman's shoe and who was subsequently indicted for conspiring to obstruct justice in the Cruz case, has taken the bench and is now the Chief Judge of DuPage County.

# 8

## THE VICTIMS

IF THESE ARE THE PERILS, why have a death penalty? What do we get out of it?

One group that consistently supports executions is the surviving loved ones of murder victims. As an AUSA, I'd handled only one shooting case. Clearly, I didn't know enough about how the world looks to the victims of violence. As a result, a number of my colleagues and I urged the Commission to hear from the murdered person's survivors, who are commonly referred to as "the victims." In murder cases, alone among crimes, the anguish and loss of loved ones stands in for what was experienced by the actual victims, who can no longer speak for themselves.

In order to sample public opinion about the capital punishment system, the Commission held open hearings in both Chicago and Springfield, the state capital. The roster of speakers was dominated by death penalty opponents, many of them associated with religious groups. (One organization whose position I hadn't anticipated was the Illinois Medical Society, which objects to state laws allowing physicians to assist in executions, in violation of the Hippocratic oath.) Understandably, survivors were not eager to turn their hearts inside out in that kind of forum, and as a result we scheduled private sessions where they felt freer to speak.

I learned a great deal in those hours. What made the deepest impression on me was my eventual recognition that losing a loved one to a murder is unlike any other blow delivered in our often-cruel lives. This is because the survivor's loss is not the result of something as fickle and unfathomable as disease, or as random as a typhoon. Instead, he has had someone ripped from him by the conscious choice of another human being. This is so far from the ingrained assumptions we share in living together that the reality is almost impossible to accommodate. And the unique nature of this loss is a special challenge to the regime of reason and rules that is the law because it exists, first and foremost, to encourage and enforce minimum standards of civilized behavior. Even before the law's technicalities, its unfamiliar language, privileges, and procedures, and its decade-long delays from trial to execution—even before all of that starts, the law, by its own terms, has failed these people.

This recognition was a long time coming to our legal system. Crime, as we conceive of it, is committed against the community as a whole, and thus matters of policy, including punishment, depend on community judgments. The U.S. Supreme Court had ruled as late as 1987, in *Booth v. Maryland*, that it was unconstitutional in a capital sentencing proceeding to admit a statement of the impact of the crime on the survivors. Such evidence was inflammatory and irrelevant, the Court said, since sentencing should look solely to the character of the defendant and his crime, not to the tears of the bereaved.

By the end of the 1980s, the so-called victims' rights movement had gained ascendance nationwide, and the Court, as has so often been the case on questions of capital punishment, reversed itself in 1991. Now, in most states, victims have a statutory right, as they do in Illinois, to be heard by the sentencing tribunal.

Do survivors want the killer to die? Not universally. But more often than not, they do. And what is it they hope to gain by seeing a murderer put to death? Obviously, answers to this question are highly individual, but in speaking to victims, certain themes emerged.

Dora Larson has been a victim advocate for nearly twenty years, helping the surviving family members deal with both the tribulations of violent crime and the way the legal system addresses it. She herself is a survivor.

"[M]y 10 year-old daughter, Victoria Joell Larson—or Vicki—was kidnapped, raped, and strangled and put into a grave her 15 year-old killer had dug three days before," she told us when she testified before the Commission on December 13, 1999. Given her professional and personal experience, Mrs. Larson was in a unique position to describe what survivors want.

[W]e survivors, our biggest fear is that some day, our child or loved one's killer will be released. And we know we never, ever get our loved one back. But we want these people off the streets so that others might

4 9

be safe. To many of us, justice means we never have to worry that our killer will ever kill again . . .

Clearly, it would render a loved one's death even more meaningless if the crime was repeated. This concern presumably can be met by a life term. Yet Mrs. Larson noted several ways in which life sentences pose a far greater emotional burden than an execution. Because Vicky Larson's killer was under eighteen, he was not eligible for the death penalty.

When I was told life, I thought it was life. Then I get a letter from the Governor that our killer has petitioned the Governor for release. And do you know, I have testified before . . . [b]ut going before that Prisoner Review Board to beg them to keep him behind bars was the toughest thing I have ever done since Vicki's funeral.

Even if we guarantee that life sentences will include no possibility of parole, anxieties remain for survivors. Another woman who appeared before us, Laura Tucker, pointed out that the man who'd savagely beaten and murdered her nine-day-old niece, the baby's father, had made two escape attempts while awaiting his death sentence. With his history of vicious child abuse, she contended that no child in the state would be safe were he again at large.

Survivors' concerns are also accelerated by the dynamism of the legal process: laws change. In Dora Larson's case, the U.S. Supreme Court's decision in *Apprendi v. New Jersey*, creating new constitutional requirements that must be met before imposing so-called enhanced sentences—

sentences that, in particularly aggravated cases, can be extended beyond the statutory maximum—has left her worrying that her daughter's killer's life term might now be unlawful. If so, his sentence could be shortened to sixty years, which would put him back on the street at the age of forty-five.

Mrs. Larson is right. As long as a killer is alive, he's likely to keep throwing paper. From a penitentiary cell, there's not much to lose. And eventually the law may come to his aid. The reality, though, is that a death sentence is probably more illusory than a life term. As I noted, even before Governor Ryan's moratorium, more than a third of the time a condemned prisoner in Illinois eventually escaped death row; and less than half of one percent had actually been executed, which is consistent with national averages. Moreover, no jurisprudence is more unstable than that governing capital sentencing. Until June 2002, the mentally retarded could be sentenced to death. Now it's unconstitutional, with no telling how many sentences across the country will be overturned as a result.

But the fact that survivors never stop hearing about the killer while he's alive motivates victim families to talk again and again about "closure," an end to the legal process that will allow them to come to final terms with their grief. Only an execution, they maintain, will provide that irreversible conclusion.

On the Commission, a number of us tried, without success, to determine whether the hope of closure is satisfied in reality. I have not found any long-range studies of survivors which attempted to assess their emotional state in the years following an execution. As Mrs. Larson said, "[S]urviving families are sentenced to a life of pain, unanswered questions, what-ifs, and trips to the grave." These remain whether the killer lives or dies. Jay Stratton, who lost his mother in the Oklahoma City bombing, watched the execution of the principal perpetrator, Timothy McVeigh. Stratton reportedly said, "I thought I would feel satisfied, but I don't." Some scholars maintain that survivors only experience more emotional turbulence in the wake of an execution.

Yet Mrs. Larson and many others assert that large numbers of survivors find the execution of their lost loved one's killer a meaningful emotional landmark. Because McVeigh had killed more than 160 people, his execution provided a broad sample of survivor opinion, and many of those who witnessed it, either in person or through a closed-circuit feed to Oklahoma City, told reporters in the immediate aftermath that they had experienced a sense of relief. There are enough such anecdotal accounts that I, for one, am unwilling to dismiss them, particularly because execution brings a definitive end point to what seems to be the most enduring grievance of many survivors.

As Dora Larson put it:

My Vicki will be 10 forever. On February 8, 2001 would be her 32nd birthday. And I am going to take a little 10 year-old Winnie the Pooh arrangement out, because she'll be 10 forever . . . [T]he victims will never see another birthday . . . [T]he inmate on condemned row has the freedom of choice. The victim had none.

The fact that a life-incarcerated killer still has birthdays, Christmases, sees the sun rise and set, can look through the visiting room panel and hear his mother say she loves him and can repeat those words to her, is the ultimate indignity to many victim families. Some critics may label the survivors' desire for death "retribution," or even "revenge," but that's subtly off the mark. From what I heard, they do not await the murderer's execution simply to establish a gruesome tit-for-tat, in which the horror of being killed is revisited on a killer, or out of the logic of the sacrificial altar, where witnessing someone else's anguish will expiate their own pain. The justice they seek is the same kind embedded in the concept of restitution: the criminal ought not end up better off than his victim. To survivors it is unconscionable and infuriating that after all the misery the murderer has wrought, he still experiences many of the small joys of existence, and thus in some measure his life and his family's is better than the victim's and theirs.

Yet even if a survivor's desire for a killer's death reflects broadly held views of what is just, the actual implementation of those wishes may not be fair. For example, emphasizing the preferences of victims has exaggerated many of the inherent inequities of our capital justice system, often enhancing the randomness of who gets sentenced to death and who does not. The murders of Melissa Ackerman and Jeanine Nicarico were virtually identical crimes, yet Brian Dugan received life imprisonment for the murder of Melissa Ackerman, because the Ackerman family was willing to accept the sure, quick resolution offered by a guilty plea, while the Nicaricos have demanded death for their daughter's killer. It violates the fundamental notion that like crimes be punished alike to allow life or death to hinge on the emotional needs of the survivors.

The rise of the victims' rights movement in the 1980s was based on the reality that survivors were often shunted aside in the criminal process, poorly informed, and even forgotten. Yet it is also not coincidental that victims' rights came into their own in the Reagan era, when there was increasing acceptance of a libertarian market-oriented ideology, which sees security as one of the few acceptable goals of government action. Building on that, the notion seems to be that when the legal system fails to provide security, citizens are entitled to assume the law's power on their own. Thus victims have sometimes become virtual proprietors of the justice system in capital cases. Yet is it the law, alone, that has failed when a murder takes place? Or is the responsibility a far broader one that reaches to all the institutions in our society—schools, churches, towns, and families? Why make the law the one engine for recompense for survivors?

To me by far the greatest fallacy in justifying capital punishment with the oft-heard mantra that "the victims deserve it" is that it is, in a favored lawyers' phrase, an argument that "proves too much"—an argument that, when extended, defeats itself. Once we make the well-being of victims our central concern and assume that execution will bring them the greatest solace, we have no principled way to grant one family this relief and deny it to another. From each victim's perspective, his loss, her anger, and the comfort each victim may draw from seeing the killer die are the same whether her loved one perished at the hands of the Beltway Sniper or died in an impulsive shooting in the course of a liquor-store holdup. The victims-first approach allows us no meaningful basis to distinguish among murders.

Yet in a state like Illinois, 49 times out of 50, a death sentence is not imposed for a first-degree homicide. Are we saying that justice has not been done in 98 percent of cases? Not according to the Supreme Court, which has established constitutional requirements that presuppose that the death penalty will be imposed on a select basis. The Court requires legislatures to create exacting guidelines about the factual circumstances under which capital punishment may even be considered, followed by a scrupulous weighing of the aggravating and mitigating factors that characterize a particular crime and defendant. And in this formulation, no matter how liberal the victim-impact rules, the expressed desires of survivors for the death penalty have no permissible role. Indeed, when we allow victims to "own" the process, we are defying that framework.

This leads me to think that we hide behind victims to some extent, identifying with their just wrath as a more comfortable expression of our own retributive impulses. Prosecutors, in particular, use the victims' desires as a fig leaf for their own judgments. When the system works as it is supposed to, however, we subordinate the survivors' wishes to other elements in our calculus of justice to determine what's best for all of us.

Nor is this wrong, in my view. While the magnitude of loss is by far the greatest for the bereaved, the community as a whole has been deprived of the victim's potential. And when we punish, we do so in the name of all of us. The unique role of the jury in expressing the will of the community is the seeming reason that American law has exalted the jury's role in capital matters, where, as in no other criminal case, it is empowered to pronounce sentence. (In acceding to this arrangement, the courts have also relieved judges of having to wield the law's most uncomfortable responsibility on many occasions.) And we don't decide what the community's interests are merely by asking victims how they feel. We know how they feel: full of grief and rage. The law ought not prolong or complicate their suffering as it tends to do—but part of that is because prosecutors and legislators make empty promises of swift and sure justice, when they know that in capital cases our jurisprudence requires saturation certainty, and thus prolonged litigation, before an execution takes place. The legal system surely owes victims an outcome that is just by common lights, so they feel no obligation to take matters into their own hands, as was portrayed in the film *In the Bedroom*. And the Commission's report pointed out that we can do a far better job in providing compassionate services for victims. Cops swarm the scene, but nobody tells the family how to get a death certificate.

Yet capital punishment defines far too much about our society and us as its citizens for us to condemn defendants to death solely for the sake of victims whose loss will never be fully erased. In a democracy, no minority, even those whose tragedies scour our hearts, should be empowered to speak for us all. Allowing survivors to rule the death penalty process makes no more sense than it would to allow only the families of the dead in the World Trade Center attack to determine what will be rebuilt on the site. At the end of the day, if we are to subscribe to the death penalty, it must benefit the rest of us, as well.

# 9

## DETERRENCE

URING THE THIRD PRESIDENTIAL DEBATE in 2000, Jim Lehrer asked both candidates whether they believed the death penalty was a deterrent.

"I do," George W. Bush answered, without disagreement from Al Gore. "It's the only reason to be for it."

Mr. Bush, so far as I can tell, was wrong on both scores. There are a number of compelling rationales for capital punishment. And deterrence, upon examination, doesn't appear to be one of them.

When I started my Commission work, I felt that if it could be established that a death sentence, as opposed to life imprisonment, actually deters other people from committing murders, it would have to weigh heavily in any candid assessment of the subject. As a result, I became an unbearable noodge to the Commission's gifted research director, Jean Templeton, who is both a lawyer and a sociologist by training, as I sought her assistance in wading through the learning in this area.

At one point, I even persuaded Jean to undertake a very informal statistical cross-comparison between Illinois and surrounding states. We ended up measuring Illinois against Michigan, and Missouri against Wisconsin, death penalty states versus non–death penalty states, pairs that had similar urban density, racial makeup, and income levels. The murder rates were higher in the death penalty jurisdictions. Indeed, Texas, which has performed more than a third of the executions in the United States since 1976, has a murder rate well above the national average. On the other hand, in the last decade, not only has the consolidated murder rate in states without the death penalty remained consistently lower than in the states that have had executions but the gap has grown wider. As a result, some sociologists have suggested that executions actually inspire murder, a so-called brutalization effect, although proof of this point is as generally unavailing as that regarding deterrence, for many of the same reasons.

Statistical cross-comparisons between states are inevitably subject to dispute. For example, many of the states that don't have the death penalty didn't have high murder rates to start; thus when murder rates drop, as they have since 1993, there might be a natural tendency for rates in the low states to drop faster. And many statistics can be argued both ways. New York reenacted its death penalty in September 1995, after the number of murders in the state had already gone into steep decline. On the other hand, New York's rates have remained low versus other jurisdictions. Is this owing to the death penalty? Proponents usually find the clearest deterrent effect from executions, and there's yet to be one in New York.

Admittedly, you can go dizzy trying to make sense of the numbers and variables, but rigorous study is still not on the side of deterrence. For example, William Bailey and Ruth Peterson, scholars who had yet to close the book on deterrence, nonetheless conceded in 1994: "Deterrence and capital punishment studies have yielded a fairly consistent pattern of non-deterrence." In 1996, Michael Radelet and Ronald Akers published a study in which they asked acknowledged experts—sixty-seven of the current and former presidents of three professional criminology organizations—whether the existing research supported a deterrence justification for capital punishment, without regard to their personal beliefs. Eighty percent said it did not. A 1995 poll by Peter D. Hart Research Associates of 386 police chiefs across the nation found that although the vast majority of them supported the death penalty for philosophical reasons, 67 percent felt it was inaccurate to say that the death penalty significantly reduces the number of homicides.

The principal academic support for deterrence has come from free-market economists, who believe that all social choices are the work of rational decision-makers responding to incentives. The economists, accordingly, have a professional interest in proving that the incrementally more severe punishment represented by the death penalty functions to prevent murder. Led by the pioneering work of Isaac Ehrlich in the mid-1970s, these scholars have developed formulas for regression analyses the length of New Jersey, quantifying every conceivable variable. The Nixon administration relied on Ehrlich's results in successfully asking the U.S. Supreme Court to reauthorize capital punishment in 1976. Yet Ehrlich and his followers have been stingingly criticized for methodological and conceptual shortcomings by other scholars, and more recent studies haven't seemed to answer objections. A 2001 paper found a deterrent effect, but the formulas employed also showed that murders are more prevalent in rural areas than in cities, a result that flies in the face of experience.

Nor does the econometric framework fully address fundamental objections to the psychological model being employed. My own impression, based on experience but little social science, is that murder is not a crime committed by those closely attuned to the real-world effects of their behavior. It's characteristic of the criminal offenders I've represented over the years, especially the young and the poor, that many seem unable even to conceive of the future. Instead, killers appear to me to act out a range of narcissistic and infantile impulses—rage, perverted self-loathing, or a grandiose conviction they'll never be caught—in which consequences have no role. Defenders of Ehrlich and his followers adhere to the numbers. If the data bear them out, they contend—for example, by showing a decline in murders in the wake of executions—their assumptions must be correct.

At the end of the day, the best I could say was this: If the death penalty is a deterrent, that fact is not visible to the naked eye. When you are asking citizens to capitulate to their government's right to kill them, you'd better be able to show them something they can understand in their own terms. Econometric models and regression analyses cannot possibly contribute much to the debate.

There is, of course, another economic argument made in behalf of the death penalty: it saves public funds, because the state does not have to provide lifetime support to an incarcerated killer. But in this, like so many other things, lawyers have a huge impact on costs.

In the United States in 2000, the average period between conviction and execution was eleven and a half years, with lawyers and courts spewing out briefs and decisions all that time. Public funds pay for almost all of this, since capital offenses are most often committed by the poor whose defenses are usually maintained at the cost of the state. There is a lot to pay for. Two lawyers at trial, one on appeal, another for the post-conviction proceedings, another for the *habeas*. And there must be prosecutors to oppose them, cops and other investigators to put the case in shape for trial, judges to hear the matter, probation officers, mitigation experts, usually a couple of shrinks, court reporters, and transcripts. And none of this considers the costs of incarceration while the convicted defendant is awaiting execution. Those on death row in Illinois and a number of other states are most often held in single cells, since a man with nothing to lose doesn't make an especially good roommate when you aggravate him. Given all those costs, researchers seem to agree that imposing the death penalty is more expensive than leaving a killer alive. A new study published in 2003, which was conducted by the gubernatorial commission in Indiana, concluded that in present values, the costs in death penalty cases exceed the total price of life without parole by more than a third.

Yet cost, I decided ultimately, is basically a red herring. Certainly cost savings don't justify capital punishment. But they do not provide a compelling argument against it, either, in most states. Capital prosecutions are relatively rare. There have been roughly ten to fifteen new death sentences in Illinois every year. Even if we imagine that the costs in those cases exceed those in a non-capital case by a million or even two million dollars, the most grandiose number used by death penalty opponents, the amount saved by abolition is small in terms of a $52.5 billion state budget. The money spent on the death penalty may have high symbolic value, but curtailing that expenditure is certainly not enough to give us a tax cut or better schools.

After two years of reading studies, I decided I wasn't going to find any definitive answers to the merits—or failings—of the death penalty in the realm of social science.

# 10

## MORAL PROPORTION: ULTIMATE PUNISHMENT FOR ULTIMATE EVIL

O N THE COMMISSION, we spent little time in philosophical debates. We were warm with one another and our discussions wandered at times, but we were busy people gathered for a serious purpose and we had no illusions we could change each other's minds. Yet to the extent that incidental exchanges occasionally got to the heart of the issue, those who favored capital punishment (and that included some of us who, at other moments, were against it, too) tended to make one argument again and again: Sometimes a crime is so horrible that killing its perpetrator is the only correct response. When everything is said and done, I suspect that the argument for what I refer to as "moral proportion" remains the principal reason why more Americans continue to support capital punishment rather than oppose it.

For me, thinking about capital punishment has always

presented the moral equivalent of Chinese handcuffs. The more insistent one is about the profound spiritual horror of the state taking a life, any life, the graver the crime becomes that occasions the punishment. Murder is a violation of another person's humanity so absolute that it is literally incomparable. Indeed, our fixation on murder in novels and film suggests our continuing inability to come to grips with it, even imaginatively.

As I've noted, the U.S. Supreme Court's lexicon, in explaining the unique procedural environment for capital cases, is that "death is different." But murder is different, too. And for this reason I've always thought death penalty proponents have a point when they say that it denigrates the profound indignity of murder to punish it in the same fashion as other crimes. These days, you can get life in California for your third felony, even if it's swiping a few videos from Kmart. Does it vindicate our shared values if the most immoral act imaginable, killing another human being without any justification, is treated the same way? For ultimate evil must there not be ultimate punishment? The issue is not revenge or retribution exactly, so much as moral order.

The death penalty in this context maintains its hold on the American conscience because of its intensely symbolic nature. Values count enormously in our lives. But it is essential to recognize that our adherence to the death penalty arises not because it provides proven tangible benefits like deterrence but rather from our belief that capital punishment makes an unequivocal moral statement.

That belief, in turn, identifies the challenge. The argument for moral proportion places an enormous burden of precision on the justice system. Every execution must be just. If we execute the innocent or the undeserving, then we have undermined, not vindicated, our sense of moral proportion and the clear message capital punishment is meant to send. Accordingly, the system has to be unfailingly accurate; it must operate with a fine-tuned sense of what ultimate evil is, and it must identify unerringly who has committed it.

I arrived on the Commission with personal experience in how poor the capital system's aim sometimes is in hitting those targets, not only in Alex Hernandez's case, but also in that of Christopher Thomas. I began representing Chris in 1996, not long after my role in the Hernandez matter was fully concluded. The story of the lawyer-author who, along with many others, had labored without charge to help free Hernandez had been popular with the press and even more so along Illinois' death row, where literally dozens of the inmates wrote me proposing I work the same magic for them. To be frank, I wasn't sure I wanted to shoulder that kind of burden again. I barely slept the week before I argued Hernandez's appeal, even though it was inconceivable that his conviction was not going to be set aside. (As it turned out, the Appellate Court's first question to the prosecution was, "Why has the state not confessed error in this case?" I.e., why can't you guys admit you made a mistake?)

More important to me, even if the percentage of innocents on death row is higher than I ever would have imagined during my years as a prosecutor, it remains the fact that the overwhelming majority of those convicted are guilty. If I was going to do this again, I wanted a case that would be less of a crusade and would instead expose me to more of the system's routine operation.

One afternoon I had assembled a group of young lawyers in my office to attend a meeting on *pro bono* death penalty work when, as a pure coincidence, I found a letter in my in-box. It was from Chris Thomas, who said he'd been convicted of first-degree murder and sentenced to death, even though none of the eyewitnesses to the crime had identified him. In a scene out of *Reversal of Fortune*, a number of the young lawyers immediately wanted to take the case. The old prosecutor in me preached caution. Several weeks later, the associates, including Brett Hart, who is now my partner, had investigated and found the letter was true—in a sense. None of the eyewitnesses had identified Thomas. However, his two accomplices had turned over on him, and with this encouragement, Chris had confessed three different times, the last occasion on videotape.

On the night of October 25, 1994, Thomas, twenty-one at the time, and his two pals had run out of gas. Everybody's stories were roughly the same. All stoned, they hatched a plan to roll somebody for money. Rafael Gasgonia, a thirty-nine-year-old Filipino immigrant, was unfortunate enough to leave the photo shop where he was employed and step out behind the strip mall for a smoke. The three grabbed Gasgonia, pulling him away from the door. Thomas held a gun on him to subdue him, but another struggle broke out and Chris fired once, instantly killing Gasgonia.

From the start I had only one question: How did a parking lot stickup gone bad end up as a capital case? The six other cases from Lake County, where the crime occurred, that had led to a death penalty were far more aggravated. Hector Reuben Sanchez was one. Alton Coleman, a notorious serial murderer, was another. There was also a double murder; a case where the defendant poisoned his parents and his grandmother-in-law; a murder where the defendant first raped the victim, then shot her five times after she reported the crime; and the murder of a sixty-three-year-old woman in which the defendant beat her with a pipe filled with concrete and then stabbed her through the heart. How did this awful but nonetheless more pedestrian killing bring Thomas to the same fate as John Wayne Gacy?

It was never completely clear to me why the Lake County State's Attorney's Office had pressed forward with this as a capital case. To be sure, Chris had a record going back to his days as a juvenile, but the incidents were more in the nature of threatened rather than actual violence—he'd just finished a stretch for discharging a firearm in public, for example. The prosecutors called Chris's crime an execution-style shooting, because the gun had been pressed close to Mr. Gasgonia's forehead, but there was no question that robbery, rather than murder, had been the plan. Perhaps the biggest factors in making the case a capital prosecution were that the state had a lot of evidence—Chris's confession, his accomplices' words, and several persons to whom Chris had admitted the murder—and Chris had nothing to give them. From conversations afterwards, it appeared to me that the State's Attorney's Office had figured they'd plead the case out eventually for a lesser sentence.

Be that as it may, the salient point is that the death penalty statute gave prosecutors the latitude to charge this "typical" murder as a capital offense. In Illinois, when our death penalty statute was passed in 1977, it listed seven factual circumstances under which a murderer would be eligible for capital punishment—killing a police officer or firefighter; killing a correctional officer or inmate; murdering more than one person; murder in the course of an air hijacking; murder of a witness; contract murder; and felony-murder, referring to an intentional murder committed by the defendant in the course of nine different forcible felonies, such as rape or armed robbery. Today there are twenty-one different ways to qualify for capital punishment in Illinois. Basically, whenever public anxieties have mounted, because of either a prominent murder or an enduring problem like gang warfare, the Illinois legislature, eager to respond to the electorate's safety concerns, has added to the list of factual circumstances under which a killer may die. Thus when Arnold Mireles, a community policing volunteer in Chicago, was killed in 1998 because of his confrontation with local landlords, the legislature made the murder of a community policing volunteer a capital offense.

Moreover, one of the original eligibility factors, felony-murder, has ballooned as well. Prosecutors love felony-murder eligibility. For one thing, it provides an avenue to a capital sentence for a violent criminal with a long record whose crime might not otherwise qualify. It allows prosecutors to sentence defendants, rather than offenses. Beyond that, felony-murder is often easier to prove than other qualification factors. The evidence that a defendant was committing an armed robbery is far more clear-cut than whether he was attempting to torture his victim with a pistol-whipping. Thus, a full 60 percent of the prisoners on Illinois' death row had arrived there thanks to felony-murder eligibility, albeit often in the company of more particular criteria.

Yet felony-murder always struck me as a logical mess.

Why should a murder in the course of a rape be death-eligible, if the same defendant could rape a woman one day and murder her for laughs the next without facing death? Does timing really make the crime any graver? More important, felony-murder by its nature aims at crimes that started out with another purpose. Aren't long-contemplated murders more aggravated than murders committed on impulse, like Thomas's?

These thoughts had not stopped the Illinois legislature, which had continued adding forcible crimes to the list of felony-murders punishable by death until they numbered sixteen. This statutory breadth vests prosecutors with great discretion about whether to seek the death penalty, and experience seems to teach that uncabined discretion, exercised by 102 different State's Attorneys, will inevitably lead to unfair results.

Chris Thomas was on death row, therefore, because of questionable legislative judgments. But in the legal system, like the rest of life, there is usually more than one reason something goes awry. Thomas, as is true of many others, was also on death row for the crime of having the wrong lawyers. He had been defended by two local private attorneys who had entered into a contract with the Lake County Public Defender's Office that paid them $30,000 per year to defend 103 cases, an average of less than $300 per matter. By contract, one assignment had to be a capital case. Ordinarily, a Deputy Public Defender experienced in capital defense was assigned with the contract lawyer, but the fiscal year was nearly over, and neither of the contract attorneys had done the required capital case, so they were assigned to the matter together. One of them had never had any role in a death penalty case; the other had only been standby counsel when Alton Coleman, already under the Ohio death sentence that led to his execution in 2002, had defended himself.

As I worked with Brett Hart and another of my partners, John Koski, our strategy was to characterize Thomas's defense in court as all you would expect for $600. In light of Chris's confessions, his trial lawyers had seemed to regard the case as a clear loser at trial and, given the impulsive nature of the murder, virtually certain to result in a sentence other than death. They did a spare investigation of Thomas's background for the inevitable sentencing hearing, an effort that was also hindered by the fact that the chief mitigation witness, Thomas's aunt, the closest thing to an enduring parental figure in his life, had herself been prosecuted on a drug charge by one of Chris's lawyers during his years as an Assistant State's Attorney. Chris's aunt distrusted her nephew's attorneys, and under her influence, Thomas soon did as well. He felt screwed around already, since he'd confessed to the crime, expressed remorse, and was rewarded for his contrition by being put on trial for his life. By the time of trial, Thomas was at war with his lawyers. He refused to discuss a guilty plea, and after he was convicted, he took the stand in his sentencing hearing to deny he committed the crime, notwithstanding his many prior confessions. Infuriated, Judge Charles Scott, who'd never sentenced anybody to death before, gave Christopher Thomas the death penalty. So the dominoes fell.

Since the time Chris's case was tried in 1995, the Illinois Supreme Court and the state legislature have taken several steps aimed at guaranteeing a competent defense in a death penalty trial. A Capital Litigation Trust Fund has been established to pay lawyers and experts, and the Illinois Supreme Court has created a Capital Litigation bar, with specific experiential requirements that both prosecutors and defenders must meet before they may try a death case.

Yet those changes do nothing to address the more fundamental problem of how prosecutors choose when to seek the death penalty. Looking over the roughly 270 reported opinions in Illinois capital cases, I was struck again and again by how random it all seemed: there were many monstrous crimes, but also a number of so-called garden-variety murders.

When the U.S. Supreme Court declared the death penalty unconstitutional in 1972 in *Furman*, the prevailing reason among the majority was because there was virtually no logic to who was being selected for execution and who wasn't. Legislatures and courts have spent the quarter century since capital punishment was restored attempting to establish more exacting guidelines and procedures, but the results are still wildly inconsistent. When Alstory Simon pled guilty to the double murder for which Anthony Porter was once nearly executed, Simon was sentenced to thirty-seven years. Chris Thomas was on death row, but other Lake County murderers whose crimes seemed far graver had escaped it, including one man who'd killed four persons; another who'd knocked his friend unconscious, then placed him on the tracks in front of an oncoming train; and a mother who'd fed acid to her baby. Where's the moral proportion in that?

Nor are the inequities that emerge in case-to-case comparisons the only troubling disparities in the application of the death penalty. Race, whose effect in capital cases is often misunderstood, provides an example of continued differential treatment. We commissioned Mike Radelet and Glenn Pierce, two leading death penalty researchers, to determine if there was any evidence that race played a part in who had been sentenced to death in Illinois since 1977. There was indeed a race effect, it turned out, but not what popular beliefs might suggest. In Illinois, according to the available records, roughly 70 percent of the persons convicted and sentenced for first-degree murder have been black (as have been more than 60 percent of the victims) and about 17 percent of the killers have been white (and about 25 percent of the victims). Once convicted, however, white murderers were sentenced to death at a rate two and one half times that for black murderers. The reason? One seems to be that the death penalty is given more frequently in the largely white, rural parts of the state. Also, in a racially divided society, whites are more likely to associate with, and thus to murder, someone white, and that— choosing a white victim—turns out to be the controlling variable. Killing a white person made a murderer three and a half times more likely to be punished with a death sentence than if he'd killed someone black.

The figures showing that death sentences are meted out far more often for murdering whites than for murdering blacks may be mitigated by various factors. Juries tend to engage in an unspoken calculation of the harm of a murder. No one would be surprised to see otherwise identical murders result in the death penalty when the victim was a beloved schoolteacher who was the mother of three young children, and a lesser sentence if the person killed was a crack-addicted drug dealer. On the face of it, race plays no part in these judgments, but because wealth, power, and status in the United States are still so unevenly distributed along racial lines, there would inevitably be a race effect, even if we were all color-blind. Furthermore, it is also fair to note that in a city like Chicago about half of murders are gang-related. Race is obviously part of the picture when we talk about gangs, but it is also significant in deciding whether capital punishment is appropriate in a given case that the victim, in messing with gangs, voluntarily placed himself in harm's way.

These factors palliate the systemic disparity, but do not seem to fully explain it. The numbers still demonstrate that race and the death penalty are linked, and suggest that the many decision-makers in the capital system—cops, prosecutors, and juries—may value white lives more highly than black ones. When the capital sentencing system places the murder of a white in the gravest classes of offenses 350 percent more often than it does the killing of a black, we are exposing potent issues, especially whether we are really punishing like crimes alike.

Examination of other variables tends to reinforce the impression that we are not. Geography, as I mentioned, also matters in Illinois. You are five times more likely to get a death sentence for first-degree murder in a rural area than would be the case in Cook County, which includes Chicago. Gender seems to count, too. Capital punishment for slaying a woman has been imposed at three and a half times the rate for murdering a man, while women are sentenced to death only 60 percent as frequently. The fact that variables like the race and gender of the victim and the location of the murder all impact on who gets the death penalty tends to call into question the notion that capital punishment vindicates a uniform or broadly shared morality, as opposed to a network of less admirable prejudices and preconceptions.

And variations related to race, locale, and gender do not take any account of the highly individualized factors that can influence the judgment of those who make the death penalty decision. The justices of the U.S. Supreme Court have debated whether the constitutional demand for consistent and reasoned imposition of capital punishment can ever be reconciled with the competing requirement that individual cases must be decided on their own peculiar facts. But the elements at play are not always limited to what aggravates or mitigates a particular matter. In one death row case with which I became familiar, defense lawyers insisted that the trial prosecutor elected capital punishment because he was leaving the State's Attorney's Office and had never tried a death penalty case. There was some circumstantial corroboration for the claim, but even if the desire for experience had only an unconscious role in the prosecutor's decision-making, it serves to emphasize how haphazard the determinative elements can be in who lives and who dies.

There are also paradoxical effects in the way sentences ultimately get carried out. Cases are sifted by the justice apparatus at widely varying rates. The tiny percentage of death row inmates who have actually been executed have been selected for that fate based on largely adventitious factors including the art of the lawyers who've represented them in post-conviction proceedings, the backlog in particular judicial systems, and the demonstrated ineffectiveness of their original lawyers. The worse the job done by the trial lawyers, both prosecutors and defense counsel, the longer condemned prisoners live, no matter how grave their crime or potent the evidence.

Standing back from it all, I found it hard to discern the guiding hand of reason. Adding these factors together—race, gender, geography, who the lawyers and jurors are, and the sheer serendipity of circumstances—one sees anything but the kind of bright-line proportionate morality the death penalty is intended to symbolize.

# 11

## REDEMPTION

THE DENOUEMENT for Chris Thomas offered lessons of its own. The matter was only in the middle innings of death penalty litigation when my partners and I started on it. Thomas had been tried, and the Capital Litigation Division of the Illinois State Appellate Defender's Office had filed an appeal for him. We began preparing the papers for the next stage, even before that appeal was resolved. The Illinois Supreme Court ruled against Chris in September 1997, and the U.S. Supreme Court denied further review the following June. In September 1998, we filed a post-conviction petition in the Circuit Court in Lake County. Basically, we cited new evidence, not considered at the trial, arguing that Chris's lawyers should have found that material, and that their oversights prejudiced Chris's case. (As I noted earlier, attacking the competence of prior counsel is, functionally, the only avenue that is open. All other issues are usually unreviewable on the theory that they should have been raised before.)

If our post-conviction petition was dismissed, or if we lost at a hearing, there would be another appeal to the Illinois Supreme Court, and, if unsuccessful, then another request to the U.S. Supreme Court for review. If all of that failed, then the post-conviction process would begin anew in federal court, with a petition for a writ of *habeas corpus*. New lawyers might well enter the case at that point, obliged to argue that I had fallen down on the job. If they lost at the trial level, they would have a federal appeal, and at least two different kinds of requests for review to the U.S. Supreme Court to look forward to, and even an attempt at a second *habeas* petition.

This procedural rundown demonstrates why many say that death penalty litigation is today's version of *Jarndyce v. Jarndyce*, unfathomably complex and unbearably protracted. Yet Chris's case offers an object lesson in why the law has developed this way. In October 1999, Judge Barbara Gilleran Johnson of the Lake County Circuit Court ruled on our petition, finding that Chris's rights were violated when the prosecutors introduced the results of a number of court-ordered psychiatric examinations against Chris in his sentencing hearing, essentially making Chris a forced witness against himself in violation of the Fifth Amendment and clear U.S. Supreme Court precedent. The judge determined that this error may have led to Chris's death sentence.

There was nothing fanciful about this ruling. The law was unambiguous, and the state did not even bother to appeal it. The fact was that the trial judge, the trial prosecutors, and Chris's trial and appellate lawyers had all glossed over a fairly obvious error. Worst of all, the Illinois Supreme Court had resolved Chris's appeal by finding that Chris had tried to exploit that psychiatric testimony, which was flatly untrue, as both the State's Attorney's Office eventually conceded and Judge Gilleran Johnson found.

None of the persons who'd made these mistakes had acted in bad faith. The body of law governing the death penalty has grown so complex that it challenges the abilities even of experts. The reason there is always further review is because there has to be, although over the years, I've sensed that the inevitability of additional scrutiny has a natural tendency to occasionally make judges and lawyers less scrupulous than the stakes would seem to require.

Reversal of Chris's death sentence was, of course, only a prelude to another death penalty hearing. My experiences in Thomas's case were antipodal to those in Hernandez's, not only because the client was guilty, but because I admired the way the prosecutors did their jobs. Mike Waller, the elected State's Attorney of Lake County (and later my colleague on the Commission), and Michael Mermel, the Chief of Felonies, defended the conviction and sentence ardently in court, but privately they maintained a willingness to hear out me and Dave Brodsky, the Lake County Public Defender, who often worked with us on the case. Notwithstanding the sharp disagreements I frequently had with the prosecutors, they approached both the law and the facts with integrity. Waller never shirked responsibility or apologized for his office's initial decisions about Chris, but he also freely acknowledged that much of the new information we brought him made the case look considerably different than it had originally.

With the help of Eileen McCarthy and Jonathan Lyon

from the Capital Litigation Division of the State Appellate Defender's Office, we had assembled a much more extensive picture of Thomas's background, and it wasn't pretty. His mother bore him when she was fifteen and she soon abandoned her child for crime and drugs. Chris had been raised in a crack house in Chicago where people came and went to buy and use narcotics. There was a lock and chain on the refrigerator, and a hole through the floor in the bathroom, which allowed you to see to the basement. Chris and other children were routinely molested. There were tales of Chris being locked in a car with attack dogs as a gang reprisal against his mother, of Chris being dropped on his head from the roof of a garage, and, the story that broke my heart, of Chris being stripped naked and searched for money by adults in the house after he had visited with his aunt in Waukegan. Considering this new information, Waller agreed that the death penalty was not appropriate. Ultimately, we settled on a sentence of one hundred years, meaning that with good behavior Chris could be released at age seventy-one.

Given my client's history, I approached his resentencing with some apprehension. If Thomas went off on a tirade about how he'd been messed around by the system, it would have no practical consequence, but it would disgust the Gasgonia family and leave a bad taste in everyone's mouth. My hope was that he would keep still, or if he was listening to my entreaties, muster the words "I'm sorry." After Judge Gilleran Johnson accepted the negotiated resolution of the case, she asked if Chris wanted to say anything.

"Yes, I would," he answered, and my heart sank. "I want to address Mr. Gasgonia's family, if they would listen."

He then turned to Rafael's mother, brother, and sister, who were seated in the spectactors' gallery, and wept as he spoke. "What I did was wrong. And I can't bring your brother back to you. No matter, no matter who I say this to, I hope that, I hope this can pay for it. I hope that you can forgive me for what happened." He then offered to meet with the family and answer any questions they had about Rafael's final moments, in the hope that it might bring them some comfort. He also apologized for not acknowledging his guilt in court years before.

I had never anticipated this kind of turnaround. Having a future, even an unbelievably distant one, had wrought an enormous change in this young man. I was under no illusions that he could now safely return to the streets and win the Nobel Peace Prize. Chris wouldn't always rise so nobly to the occasion. But his ability to stand on the same moral ground as the rest of us, to acknowledge responsibility and apologize to the family, was a triumph of a high kind for him and for the law. Leaving the courtroom, Mike Mermel, a veteran prosecutor who always seemed to see through the posing the system requires on both sides, remarked to me, "That's about as close as you get to a Hallmark moment in this kind of thing."

Thomas's turnabout after his death sentence was lifted is noteworthy, but so is the response of some prisoners to confinement. Alton Coleman, the serial killer whose murder spree terrified the Chicago area and much of the Midwest in 1984, behaved peaceably in the structured environment of the penitentiary. According to one of his lawyers, Coleman spent seventeen years in confinement without so much as a single disciplinary write-up. One of his jailers described him to the newspapers as "a model prisoner," a compliment delivered following Coleman's execution.

Personally, I have never felt the correctional system's business is social work so much as isolating the people who aren't fit to live with the rest of us. There was little basis on which to predict Chris's growth, but from all indications it soothed the Gasgonias and left most everyone feeling his life was rightly spared.

Yet once we get into the symbolic business of punishing "ultimate evil," matters such as rehabilitation and redemption inevitably become part of the calculus, since the defendant's acknowledgment of the claims of the prevailing morality lessens our need to punish in order to reaffirm those values. And once we travel that road, it becomes nigh on impossible to figure out who will be blinded by the light, and when. The only certainty is that execution will end any chance for it to occur.

# 12

## WHEN THEY MURDER AGAIN

WHEN I TALKED about abolishing capital punishment with law enforcement professionals, whether they were correctional officers, police, or veteran prosecutors, I often heard the same riposte: "Well then, what do you do about Henry Brisbon?"

In these circles, Henry Brisbon is Illinois' poster child for the death penalty. In person, it's hard to see what all the fuss is about. Brisbon looks a little like Eddie Murphy, a solidly built African American of medium height, appearing somewhat bookish in his heavy glasses. He comes across the way Murphy did playing Axel Foley in *48 Hrs.*: an amiable, quick-witted rogue greatly amused by himself. No one disputes that Brisbon is extremely bright. When I visited Henry, he had already read a great deal about the Commission on Capital Punishment and offered me predictions about which potential reforms would be roadblocked politically. His guesses were as well informed and reasonable as those of most commentators.

But the movie character Henry Brisbon most closely resembles in terms of his conduct is Hannibal Lecter. He is a veritable killing machine. Brisbon is the "I-57 murderer," a crime so infamous many Illinoisans still cringe at those words. On the night of June 3, 1973, Brisbon and three "rap partners"—his term—forced several cars off the interstate that runs south of Chicago. In one vehicle Brisbon found a woman, whom he forced to undress. He then discharged a shotgun in her vagina. From another car he rousted a young couple, compelling them at gunpoint to lie down in a field. Brisbon instructed them to "make this your last kiss," then shot both in the back.

The crimes went unsolved for years. Brisbon's role was uncovered only when he confessed to a law librarian in the penitentiary where he was serving a stretch for rape and armed robbery. By the time Brisbon could be brought to trial, the U.S. Supreme Court had declared the death penalty unconstitutional, and Brisbon was instead sentenced to 1,000 to 3,000 years, still probably the longest prison term ever imposed in Illinois.

In October 1978, eleven months after the sentencing, Brisbon murdered again. He placed a homemade knife to the throat of a guard, whom he locked in his cell, and then led several inmates to another prisoner, whom a witness said Brisbon stabbed repeatedly. The death penalty had been restored by now, and Brisbon was sentenced to be executed. The evidence in his sentencing hearing included proof of yet another murder Brisbon had allegedly committed prior to his incarceration, when he placed a shotgun against the face of a store clerk and blew him away, and of

Henry's role in leading a prisoner uprising at Stateville penitentiary in September 1979 in which several guards were assaulted.

Even after his death sentence in 1982, Brisbon has continued to compile an impressive disciplinary dossier. By now he has had over 250 disciplinary tickets, and just a small sample of his alleged misbehavior since he was first sentenced to death includes stabbing two other inmates, stabbing a guard, hitting a guard in the face with a wooden plank, and throwing a thirty-pound weight against the head of a fellow prisoner, who was seriously injured.

Brisbon is currently housed at the Tamms Correctional Center, referred to in the trade as CMAX, a "closed" maximum-security facility, and as a "Super-Max" in popular parlance. Tamms is where the worst of the worst arrive, roughly 250 bad guys culled from an Illinois prison population of almost 45,000, most of them gang leaders or men with intractable discipline problems, especially a history of attacking other prisoners or guards. Inmates remain until they have demonstrated an ability to curb their inclinations to violence. There is no indication that Brisbon will be leaving soon.

From the time I was appointed to the Commission, I requested the chance to visit Tamms, an opportunity that is extended to few outsiders. But I regarded seeing Tamms as critical. Henry Brisbon's execution might not deter other people from killing, but it will definitely keep Brisbon from murdering anyone else. Thus, the pivotal question for me was whether there were means besides execution to control the Brisbons of the world, the prisoners whose records suggest that they are so bad to the bone that they are clearly prone to murder again if given the opportunity.

If the conditions of their confinement cannot reliably prevent this, the argument in favor of capital punishment in Brisbon's case, and others like it, seems overwhelming to me. It is simply unjust to force a kind of lottery on correctional officers, doctors, nurses, and other inmates waiting to see which one of them will eventually be maimed or murdered.

So, after dozens of requests, in the spring of 2002, I was allowed to make the trip with Matt Bettenhausen and Nancy Miller, then a lawyer with the Department of Corrections, who provided continuing expertise to the Commission. Tamms is located near the bottom point of Illinois, where the state is farther south than parts of Kentucky. The Mississippi, a wide body of cloacal brown, floods the nearby lowlands, creating a green region of marshes along the orange sandstone bluffs. At the foot of one of these stone outcroppings, on twenty-six acres of a vast savanna-like grassland, stands the Tamms closed facility.

The terms of confinement in Tamms CMAX are admittedly grim. Inmates are permitted no direct flesh-to-flesh contact with other human beings. Each prisoner is held twenty-three hours a day inside a seven-by-twelve-foot block of preformed concrete, weight approximately thirty-two tons, which has a lone window to the outside, roughly forty-two by eighteen inches and segmented by a lateral steel bar. The cell contains a single stainless steel fixture holding both a toilet bowl and a sink, and a concrete pallet over which a foam mattress is laid. The door is punch plate, steel pierced by a network of half-inch circles almost like bullet holes, which permits conversation but prevents a prisoner from doing the mayhem possible when he can get his hands through the bars. Once a day, an inmate's door rolls back under remote control, and at the end of the corridor of cells, the doorway slides open, allowing exit to an outdoor area, twelve by twenty-eight feet, half of it roofed and all of it surrounded by thirteen-foot concrete walls. For an hour, the prisoner may exercise or just breathe fresh air. Showers are permitted on a similar remote-control basis, twenty minutes, several times a week.

For those who remain recalcitrant—and few do—there are still privileges that may be suspended. For example, misbehaving inmates can be put on meal loaf, which means that, rather than usual fare, they are fed a brown mass of mashed meat, spinach, and meal, among other ingredients. I sampled meal loaf and noted an undertaste of molasses. Fresh from the oven, it wasn't terrible, but several days eating nothing but this would certainly catch my attention. Prisoners who cooperate are progressively rewarded, with high favor represented by the installation of a TV, housed in a clear plastic case to prevent anyone from turning it into a weapon. (Listening to the Warden, George Welborn, describe the infractions of inmates, I was reminded again that criminality stands beside art as a testament to human imagination. Even the paranoid schizophrenics who engage in group therapy inside steel booths that resemble the isolation chambers on old TV quiz shows manage to steal the monopoly money used in their weekly games.)

Like most penal institutions, Tamms has its critics. In addition to the objections from the left that the isolation and restriction of Super-Maxes constitute cruel and unusual punishment, there are also complaints from the right. Tamms is expensive, in part because, blessedly, it is not full. The roughly $52,000 spent in 2002 on each Tamms prisoner was two and one half times the approximately $20,500 it cost on average to imprison an inmate in Illinois' other penitentiaries. You don't have to be Archie Bunker to think Henry Brisbon isn't worth it, but of the 165 or so persons on Illinois' death row at the time I visited, only 3 of them were at Tamms. In other words, execution is not an alternative for 99 percent of the prisoners at Tamms. Like other cost issues, this one does not impact in a significant way on the pro and con of capital punishment.

Instead, the ultimate question is simply this: Does it work? At Tamms, they seem to have succeeded, not merely with Brisbon but with other inmates. In 2001, among a population of the most violence-prone prisoners in Illinois, there was a total of fifty-two assaults on staff, almost all of them throwing food or excrement at guards. And of course Tamms's existence has an immeasurable effect on behavior at other institutions, since it poses a threat, even for a lifer, that there is another form of tangible punishment for serious misconduct.

The Warden at Tamms when I visited, George Welborn, is tall and lean, with a full head of graying hair, a mustache, and dark, thoughtful eyes. He speaks with the twang of southern Illinois. Welborn, who was instrumental in planning the facility, struck me throughout as a person of intelligence and decency who believes very much in the ultimate mission of corrections, which is to protect the rest of us from the inmates and the inmates from themselves. We talked about many things in the course of the day, but before we left I asked him the sixty-four-dollar question.

"Do you realistically believe, George," I said, "that you can keep Henry from killing anyone again?"

George Welborn is under no illusions about Brisbon's character. He was Assistant Warden at Stateville in 1979 when Henry had a critical role in an inmate uprising in which a number of guards were taken hostage, and as a result Welborn testified against Brisbon in the proceedings that led to his death sentence. George took his time with my question, before guardedly answering yes.

"Henry is a special case," he said when we discussed Brisbon again by phone, several weeks later. "I would be foolish to say I can guarantee he won't kill anyone again. I can imagine situations, God forbid . . . But here the chances are minimized. It's not nearly as likely as anywhere else." Welborn said he felt confident that they could keep Brisbon from fashioning homemade weapons, as Henry has done in all the other penitentiaries in which he's been held. And the Warden also believed that the design of the facility and the technology available gave the Tamms staff the means to subdue Brisbon even in the event of the unforeseen. But still, George said. Still with Henry, no one could make guarantees.

# 13

---

## THE COMMISSION'S REPORT
## AND ITS AFTERMATH

O N APRIL 15, 2002, at a crowded news conference, the members of the Commission publicly presented our report to Governor Ryan. Minutes beforehand, we had met privately with him. Paul Simon stood and praised George Ryan for his courage in declaring the moratorium. The Governor looked at Simon a moment.

"What else was I supposed to do?" he asked in his usual direct fashion, as if it had never occurred to him that he could, like so many other contemporary politicians, dismiss or ignore the errors of the capital system.

The report we handed the Governor contained eighty-five recommendations for reform. Roughly 90 percent were made unanimously. Although some members felt our most sweeping proposals went too far, we had reached a broad consensus on several points.

First, although the Capital Litigation Trust Fund and a series of rule changes implemented by the Illinois Supreme Court for death cases represented significant progress on a number of fronts, we all agreed that reform of the capital process remained essential along the line. None of the institutional players—investigators, prosecutors, defense lawyers, or judges—were functioning as well as they could. Second, we were united in believing that the death penalty had been imposed too often in Illinois. Even at a rate of one case in fifty, too many of the wrong cases had reached death row. Third, we were uniform on the need for better funding. To state it simply, if the citizens of Illinois want a system of capital punishment, they have to be willing to pay for it. Better training for police, lawyers, and judges, better defenses, better data collection—reforms we regarded as indispensable—all require more money.

Principal among the changes we urged were those aimed at lowering the risks of convicting the innocent. In response to the number of dubious confessions that appeared in the cases of the thirteen exonerated defendants, we recommended that all station house interrogations of suspects in potential capital cases be videotaped throughout. We also proposed altering lineup procedures to provide for more reliable eyewitness identifications. We urged that courts conduct pretrial hearings to determine the reliability of jailhouse informants, who often surfaced in the thirteen cases, testifying to supposed confessions in exchange for lightened sentences. To provide some minimal supervision of jury fact-finding, the Commission proposed that a death sentence not be imposed without the concurrence of the trial judge, who has heard all the same evidence as the jurors. We also suggested banning the death penalty when it is based solely on the uncorroborated testimony of a lone eyewitness or a single accomplice.

In order to lessen the seeming randomness with which some defendants end up on death row, we proposed that the twenty different eligibility criteria for capital punishment in Illinois be trimmed to five: multiple murders, murder of a cop or firefighter, murder in a prison, murder aimed at hindering the justice system, and murder involving torture. One could argue in perpetuity about which classes of murder should or should not be included, but we were unanimous that eligibility factors needed to be reduced. The list approved by a Commission majority reiterated to a great extent the original statute passed in 1977, with one major exception: felony-murder, which was the avenue that brought Chris Thomas and a number of other less worthy cases to death row, would be crossed off the list. In addition, we urged creation of a statewide oversight body, composed principally of prosecutors, to attempt to bring more uniformity to death penalty elections, so that Illinois law would be interpreted similarly in all localities, and so that decisions of individual State's Attorneys to seek execution would be subjected to limited peer review.

Finally, to ensure that the capital system is something other than an endless maze for survivors, we recommended guaranteed sentences of natural life when death is not imposed in eligible cases. In addition, we outlined reforms aimed at expediting the post-conviction and clemency processes.

Our recommendations were greeted respectfully, although hardly with universal acclaim. The major newspapers endorsed most of what we had proposed, as did the state bar association. The state prosecutors' organization, on the other hand, embraced many less far-reaching items, but dug in its heels on more fundamental reforms such as videotaping interrogations or creating a statewide review commission. Nonetheless, by appearances, there seemed to be substantial momentum for reform. All the major players—the prosecutors, the papers, even the two candidates vying to succeed Governor Ryan—supported significant changes in the capital system.

By the end of the year, none had been enacted. This was owing in part to political wrangling, but much more to the chronic timidity of politicians in taking positions that can later be labeled soft on crime. The Chair of the Illinois Senate Judiciary Committee, Kirk Dillard, eventually sponsored a legislative package produced by the Governor's staff. But the day our recommendations were issued, Dillard predicted a quick death for one of our central proposals—to reduce the number of factors for death eligibility—saying it might be "headed straight for the trash bin" because it ran contrary to the preferred political posture of legislators of both parties to expand, rather than reduce, the scope of criminal laws.

Dillard's crystal ball proved accurate. In June, I testified before a subcommittee of the Illinois Senate Judiciary Committee that was considering that proposal. Looking at his colleagues, Senator John Cullerton of Chicago pointed out to me that each of them had already run for higher office. Curbing the death penalty, he said, would give potent ammunition to future political opponents. I tried to invoke the example of Governor Ryan's courage, but the fact that the Governor didn't have enough support to run for re-election hardly helped my case. Cullerton, like Dillard, was merely brave enough to state the truth. In December, despite the Commission's recommendation to reduce the number of death eligibility factors, the Illinois General Assembly overrode Governor Ryan's veto and added a twenty-first factor for murder in the course of terrorism.

Nonetheless, the legislature's failure to act on reform only deepened Governor Ryan's predicament. In March, at a conference on the death penalty in Oregon, Ryan had remarked that he might consider commuting all death sentences in Illinois. In the wake of the Commission's report, lawyers for all but a few of the inmates on death row used our recommendations as the basis to petition the Governor to exercise his constitutional clemency powers to reduce their sentences. Throughout the fall, victims and prosecutors appeared in public hearings before the Prisoner Review Board, which considers clemency requests in the first instance. The survivors relived the gruesome facts of many of these crimes and the anguish they'd experienced, gaining widespread and sympathetic coverage. Death penalty opponents responded with a number of mediagenic events of their own, including importing stars like Richard Dreyfuss and Danny Glover for a performance of *The Exonerated*, a play telling the true stories of a number of the wrongfully convicted, before an audience that included Governor Ryan.

In dealing with the clemency issue, the Governor received no help or cover from anyone else. No one—not the legislature, the prosecutors, the candidates, or even the Commission on which I served—offered George Ryan any alternatives. He had either to accept the results of a system everyone agreed needed to be fixed or to act by himself. The latter course was not especially appealing, because as the year moved to a close, legal proceedings began in federal court in the criminal racketeering case against Scott Fawell, George Ryan's former chief of staff in the Secretary of State's Office, and against the Governor's campaign fund. In its pretrial filings, the U.S. Attorney's Office made clear that there would be testimony that the Governor might have had some role in unsavory doings. For Ryan, facing the increasing prospect that he would be in front of a jury himself, locking arms with the most unpopular minority group imaginable—convicted first-degree murderers—was not an appealing course.

But the Governor had been emphatic, especially once the Commission report detailed the long-running problems in Illinois' capital system, that he would address the cases that system had produced. Cynics claimed that in declaring the moratorium or reviewing the death row clemency petitions, Ryan was attempting to create a legacy that could compete in history books with the ignominy of the criminal conviction they saw as forthcoming. But this view of Ryan offers no explanation of other principled acts he took in this area, ones garnering him no special attention. For example, Governor Ryan twice vetoed bills that would have added new eligibility factors to the Illinois death penalty, because he regarded the statute as overly broad already.

I have no special insight into what drove George Ryan's decisions. If the government's five-year investigation of Ryan had any influence on his views about clemency, I suspect it was by providing a firsthand experience of how unfettered prosecutorial power essentially is. In my practice, I've seen federal grand jury investigations turn law-and-order conservatives into dues-paying members of the ACLU. It's even conceivable that George Ryan wanted to do the right thing as Governor because he felt he'd done wrong things in the past. Certainly I think the Governor's deep religious beliefs, which he refuses to wear on his sleeve, had a place here. Whatever the motives, though, George Ryan's refusal to duck the clemency issue despite its perils to him personally was inspiring to me, as he often was.

Initially, the Governor had spoken about a blanket clemency for all on death row. When the public hearings began, he had back-pedaled, promising the victim families he would evaluate matters case by case. After seeing *The Exonerated*, he again began to wonder aloud about clemency for all. His vacillation infuriated many observers, but I had no trouble understanding why Ryan was wrestling so fitfully with the issue.

As the time for decision drew near, reporters and others asked my opinion about what the Governor should do. I had no comment for the record, but privately I was against blanket clemency. I favored reducing sentences to life without parole in the many cases infected by the problems outlined in the Commission report. My approach would have commuted, for example, those who had been death-sentenced for felony-murder, or whose convictions rested on jailhouse snitch or accomplice testimony, or whose confessions were not well corroborated. I would have made lifers out of most, but not all, on death row, hoping to show some deference to the popular will in favor of capital punishment. I feared that a blanket commutation might inspire a powerful backlash that would scuttle all hope for reform. As an attorney, I also worried that the reliability of the law as an institution could be brought into question when the work of many years by police, prosecutors, judges, and juries—as well as the implied promise to victims' families—was overturned because of the beliefs of a single individual, no matter how well intentioned.

On the Friday before he left office, January 10, 2003, Governor Ryan pardoned four men on death row on grounds of innocence. Their cases had all come out of Chicago's Area Two Violent Crimes station house in the 1980s, where evidence introduced in a police disciplinary hearing and an ensuing federal civil rights trial had been found to show that the commander, Jon Burge, had approved extracting confessions from suspects through systematic torture—electric shock to the genitals, placing typewriter covers over defendants' heads to deprive them of oxygen, burnings, beatings, forced games of Russian roulette, and hanging suspects from handcuffs. In all four pardoned cases, the principal evidence against the defendant was a confession, which each man maintained Area Two officers had used torture to obtain. Aaron Patterson, a gang leader with a history of serious violence, had contended, since his first court appearance, that he had confessed only after twenty-five hours of physical abuse that included beatings and placing a plastic bag over his face. At one point, he said he had found a paper clip, and on a bench where he'd briefly been left alone, etched a dated message reading, "I lied about murders / Police threatened me with / violence, slapped and / suffocated me with plastic." The words were later found—and photographed—by an investigator from the Public Defender's Office.

The Governor's pardons brought to seventeen the total number of those sentenced to death in Illinois and later exonerated. But that still left the question of what to do with all the others on death row. After favoring broad but partial clemency, I'd gradually come to recognize the problems with that approach, especially as I began considering how it could be applied in given cases. Deciding on a reasoned basis who would live and who would die was, as ever, virtually impossible.

Surely, if there was a case to execute anyone, Henry Brisbon, the inmate I'd visited at Tamms, who is probably the most dangerous man in the Illinois prison system, would seem to stand at the top of the list. Yet in the days since Brisbon was first sentenced to death for stabbing an inmate, two prisoners who testified against him, the only eyewitnesses who'd seen Brisbon approach or assault the victim, had both recanted, providing affidavits stating that they lied in response to threats and promises from prosecutors. True, they are convicts, who might have many motives to change their stories—but the state had been willing to take their word at trial, even though both had initially claimed to know nothing about the murder. There was other evidence against Brisbon: his fingerprint was found beneath the tape on the handle of the knife that was probably the murder weapon, leaving little doubt that he was its manufacturer. Given this, I have no question that the evidence against Brisbon supported his conviction. But no one can possibly rest easy with an execution where the only eyewitnesses are jailhouse snitches whose stories have changed often and who now say prosecutors got the wrong man.

And yet, if you do not execute Henry Brisbon, who in good conscience can be executed? Again and again, the cases that seemed to present the most compelling facts favoring execution proved, under scrutiny, to have elements that raised second thoughts. Kenneth Allen murdered two police officers in 1979, but a portion of his brain had been removed in 1972. He has been in a mental institution for more than two decades. Latasha Pulliam and her boyfriend sexually abused a six-year-old girl with a shoe polish applicator and a hammer, and then strangled her. But Pulliam's death sentence contrasts with the life sentence the boyfriend received; and there is evidence that Pulliam is retarded, which, if sustained, would prohibit her execution anyway. Andrew Johnson committed a gruesome armed robbery and stabbing to earn a death sentence, but his co-defendant, who stabbed another victim and hit a third with a fireplace tool, got forty years.

Frustrated by the impossibility of picking and choosing among cases on any principled basis, Governor Ryan has said he ultimately decided against "playing God." On Saturday, January 11, at Northwestern's Center for Wrongful Convictions, where Larry Marshall had spearheaded the legal fight that led to the exoneration of so many of those 17, George Ryan commuted the sentences of the 167 persons left on death row. He reduced 3 sentences to 40 years, bringing them into line with what co-defendants in the cases had received. The 164 others were commuted to life in prison without parole.

Given what faced him, I think George Ryan made an understandable choice, even though such men as Henry Brisbon and Hector Sanchez, the killer of Michelle Thompson, now will not die. Lost in the ensuing furor was the fact that in everyday terms nothing had changed for the 164 prisoners commuted to life. They were in the penitentiary the day before their commutation. They would be in the penitentiary the day after. And they would still be in the penitentiary the day they died.

In 1994, as his years on the U.S. Supreme Court were approaching an end, Justice Harry Blackmun expressed his frustrations with the dizzying and persistent inequities of a capital system that, in his view, had defied all the efforts he'd supported over the decades to rationalize it. "From this day forward, I no longer will tinker with the machinery of Death," Justice Blackmun wrote, in a famous dissent. "The basic question—does the system accurately and consistently determine which defendents 'deserve' to die?—cannot be answered in the affirmative . . ."

In commuting all of Illinois' standing death sentences, Governor Ryan quoted Justice Blackmun. He had reached the same point. But unlike Justice Blackmun, Governor Ryan had the one vote that counted.

The reaction to Governor Ryan's commutations in many regards defied predictions. A number of prosecutors, police officers, and survivors expressed outrage, but the public mood was far calmer than I, for one, had anticipated. In February, the *St. Louis Post-Dispatch*, a newspaper that serves much of southern Illinois, published poll results showing that Illinoisans were essentially evenly divided about whether the former Governor had done the right thing. Although 55 percent of the poll respondents still favored the death penalty, only 29 percent said they did so "strongly." Even more impressive to me, given the skittishness I'd encountered among legislators, was this result: 65 percent of those polled said they were not likely to vote against a representative who favored abolition. Clearly, recent history had had a formative impact on opinion in my state.

Furthermore, the fact that roughly half the state agreed with their former Governor suggested that many in Illinois were sympathetic to the argument George Ryan had made in granting clemency, namely, that he had been left with little choice because the legislature had failed to enact any kind of reform. Rather than prompting the backlash I feared, George Ryan's clemencies end up spurring the Illinois General Assembly, now in control of a Democratic majority, at last to make changes in Illinois' death penalty system. In March 2003, a bill to abolish the death penalty actually received a favorable vote from a House committee before dying on the House floor. Yet the withering away of that effort occurred only as both the Illinois House and the Senate passed reform legislation, embodying a number of measures rooted in the Commission's proposals. One bill mandated videotaping interrogations in homicide cases. A second, broader reform measure sponsored by Senators Cullerton and Dillard, among others, passed both houses in late May 2003 and embodied many more of the Commission's most prominent recommendations. The reform bill called for hearings prior to the testimony of in-custody informants in capital cases, pilot programs to test the new lineup procedures the Commission favored, easier access for defendants to DNA testing after trial, and limiting felony-murder to inherently violent felonies. The measure also established procedures that would bar capital punishment if a court found the conviction was based solely on the uncorroborated testimony of an informant, accomplice, or eyewitness. It provided for decertification of law enforcement officers who willfully lie in homicide cases, and established procedures for determining whether a defendant is mentally retarded, presumptively barring capital punishment for those with an IQ of 75 or less.

Naturally, I would have liked even more, especially a state commission to approve death penalty cases, but prosecutors continue to insist that such a measure would be unconstitutional. I was disappointed that the bill still left Illinois with 21 death-eligibility factors. And factual review of guilty verdicts in death cases would remain limited under the new legislation. Trial judges may state their reasons for disagreeing with a death verdict, but not to overturn it; the law, though, would give the Supreme Court the power to set aside any death sentence it deemed "fundamentally unjust."

Nonetheless, taken as a whole, the measures would constitute important vindication for the work of the Commission and for Governor Ryan and would clearly enhance the quality of capital justice in Illinois. Early in May the new Governor, Rod Blagojevich, promised to sign the videotaping bill. Without making a final commitment, Governor Blagojevich also spoke favorably about the broader reform package when it passed at the end of the month.

Most remarkable to me was the altered political landscape. The omnibus reform bill passed the Illinois House in a vote of 117–0, and the Senate 56–3. Reform notwithstanding, Governor Blagojevich, who had run to succeed George Ryan supporting capital punishment, said, through a spokesman, that he had no intention of lifting the moratorium "anytime soon" and indicated that it might well remain in place throughout his term. Blagojevich has said there will be no executions until he is certain that the innocent can no longer be sent to death row and until there has been further review of "social inequities" that are part of the capital system. His remarks irked a few conservative legislators, but there was no widespread furor. For the time being, the lessons, the labor, and the turmoil of the last few years seem to have left Illinoisans content to see the death chamber continue to gather dust.

# 14

## WRITING ABOUT THE DEATH PENALTY:
## *REVERSIBLE ERRORS*

WHEN MATT BETTENHAUSEN, the Deputy Governor, had first spoken to me about joining the Commission, I said there was one complication: I had already begun work on a novel with capital punishment as its theme. Thinking it through, neither Matt nor I could see why that would pose what lawyers would recognize as a conflict of interest. In the end, though, my commitment to myself was that I wouldn't publish that book until the Commission had made its report to the Governor. I knew that the novel would bring questions from reporters about my views on capital punishment, and I was reluctant to offer any opinions while the Commission's deliberations, which were confidential, were under way.

The book I was working on, *Reversible Errors*, was published in October 2002, six months after the Commission report was issued. I had always said I would never write a novel about Cruz and Hernandez. The experience was too loaded, and I didn't want anyone to think I was exploiting a case I'd taken on for free. More important, it wasn't what I think of as my kind of story. As I saw it then—and see it even today—Cruz and Hernandez is a tale of good guys and bad guys. On one side was the cadre of virtuous defense lawyers, supported by earnest journalists and honest cops, who passed these cases to one another like a torch over more than a decade, convinced of the innocence of these men and working for little or no compensation. On the other side were a number of prosecutors and police officers whose reluctance to admit their errors, for fear of the damage to their own self-esteem or ambitions, drove them to ever graver mistakes.

Goodness in this world is rarely divided so definitively. In the law, especially, things are usually a muddle. Most often, there are well-intentioned people on both sides of a case. Over the years, the actual experiences I'd had began to transform themselves imaginatively, so the new cast of characters I saw in my head appeared without white hats or black. Once that happened, I began to feel the vibration of something I might like to write about.

The plot of *Reversible Errors* draws only superficially on Alex's case. Rommy Gandolph is thirty-three days away from execution for a triple murder when Arthur Raven, a former prosecutor now a corporate lawyer, is unwillingly appointed by the federal appellate court to administer what Arthur regards as the legal equivalent of last rites. In time, though, Arthur discovers that a dying prisoner in the penitentiary where Gandolph is housed is prepared to admit that he, not Gandolph, committed the murders.

Besides Arthur, there are three other main characters. Muriel Wynn, the prosecutor who sent Gandolph to death row, is now about to run for the top prosecutor's job. She is personally ambitious, but also highly capable and earnestly committed to the murder survivors. Along with Larry Starczek, a bright detective who originally investigated the case, Muriel regards the new deathbed confession as the usual jailhouse hokum. Gillian Sullivan, a disgraced former judge who sentenced Gandolph to death, has now only recently been released herself from the penitentiary where she had been sent for taking bribes; she finds Gandolph's case oddly symbolic of the mistakes in her own life. As their creator, I felt a divine love for all of these characters, which included an appreciation of their foibles and their heroic aspects.

When I started *Reversible Errors* in 1999, I'd had one point of departure imaginatively: the intense passions these cases always roil up for all the participants in the legal proceedings. At the core was my recollection of the anger and the burden I experienced in representing someone facing an unjust sentence, and the contrasting sense of high purpose I'd felt when I was a prosecutor. Early on in the book, the novel recounts Arthur's reflections about the world of criminal law and capital prosecutions, which the court's appointment has forced him to reenter:

Since leaving the Prosecuting Attorney's Office, Arthur had played defense lawyer infrequently, only when one of the firm's corporate clients or its bosses was suspected of some financial manipulation. The law he lived most days as a civil litigator was a tidier, happier law, where both sides fudged and the issues raised were minuscule matters of economic policy. His years as a prosecutor seemed to be a time when he'd been assigned each day to clean out a flooded basement where coliform bacteria and sewer stink rotted almost everything. Someone had said that power corrupted. But the saying applied equally to evil. Evil corrupted. A single twisted act, some piece of gross psychopathology that went beyond the boundaries of what almost anybody else could envision—a father who tossed his infant out a tenth-floor window; a former student who forced lye down the throat of a teacher; or someone like Arthur's new client who not only killed but then sodomized one of the corpses—the backflow from such acts polluted everyone who came near. Cops. Prosecutors. Defense lawyers. Judges. No one in the face of these horrors reacted with the dispassion the law supposed. There was a single lesson: things fall apart. Arthur had harbored no desire to return to that realm where chaos was always imminent.

When I wrote that paragraph, relatively early in the scattered process in which I work toward a first draft, I knew I'd expressed the novel's central vision. But I would have been hard pressed to articulate more. Writing, for me, when it's best, is conducted at remove from my cerebral life. The moment when I first truly believed I was destined to become an author occurred in my junior year of college when I climbed out of a fever bed and in twelve hours wrote a solid draft of a short story I later published. Writing in the grip of emotion, attempting to assign words to onrushing feeling, remains the central experience for me. In the initial stages, I seldom reflect at great length on the meanings of the action I envision. I strive to create a coherent imagined world. If that emerges, there will be a wholeness in the novel in which significance is implicit. Generally speaking, I think fiction seeks to reflect the ambiguity and contradictions in experience, not some slogan or message. If there were a shorter way to fully express what the story does, there would be no point in telling it.

Certainly, I did not want to write a dogmatic book about the death penalty, because, as I have confessed at length here, my feelings about capital punishment were anything but firm. I wanted only to portray the maelstrom of emotions that swirls within each of the warring contenders on the legal battlefield.

As a result, there was a strange companionship between my lawyerly work on the Commission—reading learned papers and court cases, writing reports and framing rules— and the emotionally engrossing but less analytical work on the novel. For the most part, I was convinced that the two enterprises did not intersect. And as a result, I was not conscious of exactly what the imaginative living-through with my characters of Rommy Gandolph's case was contributing to my reflections about capital punishment.

In retrospect, though, I think I was settling on some insights that would contribute to my ultimate conclusions. Reason, in my novel, battles not only the strong emotions provoked by a horrendous crime but also the giddiest impulse—love. In fact, many readers and reviewers commented that *Reversible Errors* is more a love story than a tale of courtroom proceedings. Arthur, Rommy's lawyer, and Gillian, once Rommy's judge, end up an item, as Larry, the detective, and Muriel, the prosecutor, were a decade before. The complications between men and women are hardly a new theme for me—or for the novel. But, as is my custom, I did not reflect at length on why the book makes such a dogged contrast between the legal case that consumes these characters and their desperate pursuit of emotional connection in their personal lives. Now that the novel is behind me, the point seems relatively clear.

In confronting murder, we as a society ask how we should face an ultimate evil, which, if unchecked, would reduce almost all human interaction to war. We want to punish in order to prevent murder, but also as part of our effort to restore ourselves from the anxieties it raises about our ability to live with one another. I have always suspected that what we want most from punishment, beginning with the moments when we first hit someone back as young children, is restoration. The pain will leave us and go instead into the person we hurt. Given that, I have occasionally wondered as I've listened to the surviving family of murder victims if, in some shadowed place in their heart, is the hope that the death of the killer will somehow restore their lost loved one to life.

Even to state all of these goals is to recognize their impossibility. The legal process will never fully heal us. The failure of the law to deliver all that we ask from it is probably the essential theme of all of my novels, and even of the one earlier nonfiction book I wrote about being a law student. I revere the enterprise of the law, but it does not function flawlessly. It neither finds the truth nor dispenses justice with the reliability it is obliged to claim. The law's sharp-edged rules never cut through the murk of moral ambiguity, nor do they fully comprehend or address the complexities of human motivation and intention. And just punishment alone does not render the world one we want to live in.

Murder takes us to the Land's End of the law. Our horror and revulsion undermine our capacity to reason—and prove that justice alone will not make us whole. Only the attachments we have to each other, the antipodal experience of what goes on in the moment a murderer kills, can accomplish that. In the face of the cruelties we visit upon one another, murder being the gravest wrong among them, a sense of meaning and connection must come from outside the law.

# 15

## CONCLUSIONS

W HEN I'D GONE DOWN TO TAMMS with Matt
Bettenhausen and Nancy Miller and met
Henry Brisbon, I'd had a subordinate reason
for making the trip: Illinois' execution chamber is now located there. Unused for more than two years because of
Governor Ryan's moratorium, it remains an irretrievably
solemn spot, with the sterile feel of an operating theater in
a hospital, replete with stainless steel tables and the blank
window of an observation gallery. The execution gurney
where the lethal injection is administered is covered in a
starched sheet and might even be mistaken for an examin-
ing table, but for the arm paddles that extend from it, and
the criss-crossing leather restraints that strike a particularly
odd note in the world of Tamms, where virtually all other
materials are steel, concrete, and plastic.

Several years ago, I attended a luncheon where Sister

Helen Prejean, author of *Dead Man Walking*, delivered the keynote address. The daughter of a prominent New Orleans lawyer, Sister Helen is a powerful orator in her own right. Inveighing against the death penalty, she looked at the audience and repeated one of her favorite arguments: "If you really believe in the death penalty, ask yourself if you're willing to inject the fatal poison."

Standing in the death chamber at Tamms, I had Sister Helen in mind. It is an illusion to think that jailers themselves don't find an execution deeply unsettling. George Welborn pointed out that one advantage of having the execution chamber at Tamms, away from the vast majority of death row inmates, is that it avoids asking correctional officers to help terminate the life of someone they have lived with every day, albeit in the relationship of guard and guarded. When we discussed the possible outcomes of the Commission's work, George, who had presided over lethal injections before the moratorium, looked at all of us and said, "If I don't have to do another execution ever again, that's fine with me."

We went from the death chamber to the cell of Ike Easley, a former gang leader who received a capital sentence for performing a revenge killing on a correctional officer. Easley is not a letter from home. The evidence at his sentencing hearing years ago showed that while imprisoned he had six reports for assault, thirty for insolence or threats, fifty-two for disobeying orders, sixty-four for unauthorized movement, three for gang activity, four for dangerous contraband, and two for drugs and paraphernalia. But standing behind the punch plate of his cell, Easley seemed slow-witted and eager to please. Even knowing his record, I was struck by the cruelty of executing someone like this, who has been rendered docile and subdued. The horror of a cool, contemplated end to the life of another human being, especially in the name of the law, is profound.

And yet, if it were Gacy, the murderer of thirty-some young men, on that gurney, if circumstance had put me in George Welborn's position, I could, as Sister Helen would have it, push the button. After two years of solemn contemplation, I won't pretend that I think the death penalty is the product of an alien morality, or that I can't respect the considered judgment of the greater portion of my fellow citizens that it ought to be imposed on the most horrific crimes.

Recognizing that capital punishment still commands a political majority in Illinois, the Commission proceeded on the assumption that the death penalty would continue, and confined our formal recommendations to prospective reforms. Yet, as Senator Simon promised he would do from the start, he nonetheless called on us as thoughtful persons who had now studied this issue at length to give the people of the state of Illinois our best advice, as an expression of sentiment rather than a formal proposal. Should capital punishment continue to be imposed in Illinois? On a day late in the fall of 2001, as we were preparing for a dinner with the Governor at the Executive Mansion in Springfield, Paul called the question and asked for a vote. A majority said no to capital punishment. A number of the Commission members who had been unwilling to declare themselves opponents of death penalty when we started, had, after two years of digesting cases and research, crossed that fateful Rubicon to say they were against killing killers. Some had moral objections. Some thought the death penalty was a waste of scarce resources. Some thought that the proposals we'd made, which were essential to true re-form, would never be fully adopted by the Illinois General Assembly and that abolition was the only sensible alterna-tive, as a result.

Although the ebb and flow of American opinion about capital punishment will continue for decades, I suspect that the death penalty will eventually be abolished in this coun-try. The world community seems intent on shaming us for adhering to a practice it regards as savage, and as globaliza-tion proceeds, those opinions are likely to count for more here. Indeed, there are even increasing numbers of conser-vatives with growing doubts, calling capital punishment one more government program that has failed, or blaming death penalty opponents for making the process so time-consuming and expensive that it is not worth the struggle.

But it is not political consensus that is likely to take us to abolition. I expect Americans—and their politicians—to remain in conflict, provoked by individual cases and reluc-tant to focus on the actual output of the system as a whole. Their hesitation to fix what is fixable in our capital schemes will force the ultimate judgments into the courts. The incremental approach the U.S. Supreme Court has fa-vored for the last twenty-five years, creating strict proce-dural hurdles to death sentences and declaring the death penalty unconstitutional in more and more settings—when applied to the mentally retarded; when decided, after a ver-dict, by a judge—will eventually stretch the fabric of the law to the point that it is too much of a patchwork to be regarded as a work of reason. Because of this, there may be intervals when the Court attempts to tamper no further with capital punishment. But the gross inequities that these extreme cases routinely seem to produce will not allow the Court to keep its distance forever. While the framers clearly accepted death as a permissible punishment, they also accepted slavery and the chattelizing of women. Times change. Eventually, I expect the Court to conclude that capital punishment and the promise of due process of law are incompatible.

I admit I am still attracted to a death penalty that would be available for the crimes of unimaginable dimensions like Gacy's, or that would fully eliminate the marginal risks that incorrigible monsters like Brisbon might ever again satisfy their vampire appetites. But if my time on the Commission taught me one lesson, it was that I was approaching the question of capital punishment the wrong way. There will always be cases that cry out to me for ultimate punishment. That is not the true issue. The pivotal question instead is whether a system of justice can be constructed that reaches only the rare, right cases, without also occasionally condemning the innocent or the undeserving.

Thus, for me, at the end of the day, the question is which mistake I prefer to see made by this system that has long symbolized our moral instincts as a nation. Allowing Gacy or Brisbon to live is infuriating, even shaming when the law must tell the survivors that their taxes will help finance the continued existence of such men. But the furious heat of grief and rage the worst cases inspire will inevitably short-circuit our judgment and always be a snare for the innocent. And the fundamental equality of each survivor's loss, and the manner in which the wayward imaginations of criminals continue to surprise us, will inevitably cause the categories for death eligibility to expand, a slippery slope of what-about-hims. After twenty-five years of attempting to establish laser-like guidelines, we still end up with a moral hodgepodge where Chris Thomas is condemned to die because he is poor and belligerent, while the likes of the Menendez brothers, who shotgunned their parents for their millions, or the Unabomber, who killed and maimed and threatened the nation for years, get life. In yet another of the perpetual paradoxes in this subject, retaining the death penalty seems to be a road to breeding disrespect for the law, because it exposes so many of its shortcomings.

One reason our capital jurisprudence is such a mess is because even the justices of the U.S. Supreme Court, who have long experience in making and sticking with hard decisions, have waffled. Harry Blackmun is hardly alone. In the last twenty-five years, Justices Stewart, White, Powell, and Stevens have also taken varying positions when confronted with the question of whether or not capital punishment as currently practiced is constitutionally tolerable. I take myself as no better than they. Long after that day in fall 2001, when Senator Simon called upon us all to offer a definitive judgment on the death penalty, a number of my fellow commissioners revised their positions. But I appear to have finally come to rest on the issue. Today, I would still do as I did when Paul Simon asked whether Illinois should retain capital punishment. I voted no.

*Preamble to the Report of the Illinois*

*Governor's Commission on Capital*

*Punishment, April 2002*

———

*Notes*

————————

*Acknowledgments*

*Below is the Preamble to the Commission's Report, summarizing our major recommendations. While I wrote an initial draft, most Commission members, and a number of the staff, made significant contributions to what appears here.*

## PREAMBLE

ON MARCH 9, 2000, shortly after declaring a Moratorium on executions in Illinois, Governor George Ryan appointed this Commission to determine what reforms, if any, would ensure that the Illinois capital punishment system is fair, just and accurate. Today, we are presenting the Governor with our recommendations. Most of these proposals were endorsed unanimously by our Commission. Although individual members of the Commission disagree with some specific proposals, the Commission members are uniform in their belief that the body of recommendations as a whole would, if implemented, answer the Governor's call to enhance significantly the fairness, justice and accuracy of capital punishment in Illinois.

Our deliberations were the product of 24 months of

intensive collaboration and research. Consistent with the Governor's original mandate, we carefully scrutinized the cases of thirteen Illinois defendants who have been released from death row in recent years after their convictions were invalidated. We also studied all reported capital decisions in Illinois, whether the death sentence or the underlying conviction was under review. We held public and private sessions where we heard from the surviving family members of murder victims, and from opponents of the death penalty, including some of the defendants who had been released from death row. We consulted with many nationally recognized experts in fields of study related to capital punishment, and we commissioned and conducted studies of our own. We also considered recommendations from across the country made by a number of bodies similar to our own, formed to consider potential capital punishment reforms. In all, our purpose was to thoroughly examine all aspects of the justice system as it relates to capital sentences and to become familiar with the research and learning in this area.

Despite the diversity of backgrounds and outlooks among those on the Commission, we are unanimous in many of our conclusions. All members of the Commission believe, with the advantage of hindsight, that the death penalty has been applied too often in Illinois since it was reestablished in 1977. Accordingly, we are unanimous in agreeing that reform of the capital punishment system is required in order to enhance the level of scrutiny at all junctures in capital cases. All Commission members also agree that if capital punishment is to continue to be imposed in Illinois, achieving a higher degree of confidence in the outcomes will require a significant increase in public funding at virtually every level, ranging from investigation through trial and its aftermath. We all also believe that significant reforms to the capital punishment system have taken place already, through legislation creating the Capital Litigation Trust Fund and through the Illinois Supreme Court's promulgation of extensive new rules governing many aspects of capital trials.

Ordering our proposals according to the procedural stage to which they apply, the following is a summary of some of our specific recommendations:

### A. Investigation:

1. We recommend videotaping all questioning of a capital suspect conducted in a police facility, and repeating on tape, in the presence of the prospective defendant, any of his statements alleged to have been made elsewhere.

2. Recognizing an increasing body of scientific research relating to eyewitness identification, we propose a number of reforms regarding such testimony, including significant revisions in the procedures for conducting line-ups.

### B. Eligibility for the Death Penalty

3. The Commission unanimously concluded that the current list of 20 factual circumstances under which a defendant is eligible for a death sentence should be eliminated in favor of a simpler and narrower group of eligibility criteria. A majority of the Commission agreed that the death penalty should be applied only in cases where the defendant has murdered two or more persons; or where the vic-

tim was either a police officer or a firefighter; or an officer or inmate of a correctional institution; or was murdered to obstruct the justice system; or was tortured in the course of the murder.

4. We also have recommended that the death penalty be barred in certain instances because of the character of the evidence or the defendant. We recommend that capital punishment not be available when a conviction is based solely upon the testimony of a single eyewitness, or of an in-custody informant, or of an uncorroborated accomplice, or when the defendant is mentally retarded.

C. *Review of the Prosecutorial Decision to Seek the Death Penalty:*

5. In order to ensure uniform standards for the death penalty across the state, we recommend that a local state's attorney's decision to seek the death penalty be confirmed by a state-wide commission, comprised of the Attorney General, three prosecutors, and a retired judge.

D. *Trial of Capital Cases:*

6. We have proposed a number of additional measures to augment the reforms already adopted by the Illinois Supreme Court to enhance the training of trial lawyers and judges in capital cases. Included are our suggestions for increased funding.

7. We have offered several recommendations aimed at intensifying the scrutiny of the testimony of in-custody informants, including recommending a pretrial hearing to determine the reliability of such

testimony before it may be received in a capital trial.

8. To allow for future audits of the functioning of the capital punishment system, we also suggest that a designated array of information about the nature of the defendant and the crime be collected by the trial court.

## E. Review

9. We recommend that when a jury determines that death is the appropriate sentence in a case, the trial judge, who has also heard the evidence, must concur with that determination, or else sentence the defendant to natural life.

10. We recommend that, as in several other states, the Illinois Supreme Court review each death sentence to ensure it is proportionate, that is, consider whether both the evidence and the offense warrant capital punishment in light of other death sentences imposed in the state.

Because capital punishment is presently lawful in Illinois and because it appears to have the support of a majority of Illinois citizens, our deliberations have concentrated primarily on these reforms and other proposals, rather than on the merits of capital punishment. Only at the close of our work did we consider that question. A narrow majority of the Commission would favor that the death penalty be abolished in Illinois. Those favoring abolition did so either because of moral concerns, because of a conclusion that no system can or will be constructed which sufficiently guarantees that the death penalty will be applied without arbitrariness or error, or because of a determination that the social resources expended on capital punishment outrun its benefits. Some members voted that we recommend to the Governor that should the Governor conclude, after studied and supportable analysis, that the legislature will not substantially implement the recommendations of this Report, that the Moratorium on the death penalty continue and that the death penalty be abolished in the State of Illinois. A slightly smaller number of Commission members concluded that the death penalty should continue to be applied in Illinois. Those favoring the death penalty believe it retains an important role in our punishment scheme in expressing, in behalf of the community, the strongest possible condemnation of a small number of the most heinous crimes. All members of the Commission have emerged from our deliberations with a renewed sense of the extraordinary complexities presented by the question of capital punishment.

Our divergence on that ultimate question was not unanticipated in light of the varied viewpoints and experience among those whom the Governor chose to serve on the Commission. What is more noteworthy, we believe, is the consistency of judgment among us about how our capital punishment system can be improved. The Commission's discussions have been characterized by an amity and respect for the differences among members, which is, frankly, extraordinary given the sharp divisions that capital punishment has traditionally provoked in the United States. In assessing our work, we are proudest of the broad agreements we have been able to achieve. A strong consensus emerged within the Commission that if capital punishment is retained in Illinois, reforms in the nature of those we have outlined are indispensable to answering the Governor's call to better ensure a fair, just and accurate death penalty scheme.

We anticipate careful reflection about these proposals by the Governor, the legislature, and Illinois citizens at large. Whatever their ultimate conclusions, all members of the Commission have been deeply honored by the opportunity to serve and to contribute to public discussion of so difficult and significant a subject.

April 2002

# NOTES

This book is a personal reflection, informed more by experience than study, and, as such, is not to be mistaken for a work of scholarship. The following notes are offered solely for the curious, to substantiate the many assertions of fact in the text. In identifying judicial opinions, I have followed accepted legal citation, except for allowing myself the pleasure of abandoning the meaningless anachronism of including mention of a higher court's denial of further review. Web citations were accurate at press time.

3 *On February 3, 1984*: The details of Hector Sanchez's crimes are reported in three Illinois Supreme Court decisions captioned *People v. Sanchez*, 115 Ill. 2d 238, 503 N.E.2d 277, 104 Ill. Dec. 720 (1986); 131 Ill. 2d 417, 137 Ill. Dec. 629, 546 N.E.2d 574 (1989); 169 Ill. 2d 472, 662 N.E.2d 1199, 215 Ill. Dec. 59 ( 1996); and a Wisconsin case, *State v. Sanchez*, 149 Wis. 2d 763, 441 N.W.2d 756 (Wisc. Ct. Appls., Dist. 1, 1989).

5 *"The Case That Broke Chicago's Heart"*: The published opinions of the Illinois Supreme Court set forth much of the story of Buckley, Hernandez, and Cruz. *People v. Hernandez*, 121 Ill. 2d 293, 521 N.E.2d 25, 117 Ill. Dec. 914 (1988); *People v. Cruz*, 121 Ill. 2d 321, 521 N.E.2d 18, 117 Ill. Dec. 907 (1988); *People v. Cruz*, 162 Ill. 2d 314, 643 N.E.2d 636, 205 Ill. Dec. 345 (1994) [hereafter *"Cruz* II"]. The 1995 unpublished opinion of the Illinois Appellate Court's Second Judicial District, reversing Hernandez's conviction in the case I argued in his behalf, *People v. Hernandez* (No. 2-91-0940) (Ill. App. Ct. 1/30/95) [hereafter *"Hernandez* II"], is posted at *http://www.scottturow.com/ultimatepunishment*, along with the brief Matt Tanner, Leslie Suson, and I filed for Alex [hereafter *"Hernandez* Brief"]. A comprehensive account of the Cruz and Hernandez cases from the initial investigation to the eventual indictment of several DuPage County officials involved in the prosecution is contained in T. Frisbee and R. Garrett, *Victims of Justice* [hereafter *Victims*] (Avon, 1998).

5 *A few days before the primary . . . indicted*: The atmosphere surrounding the initial indictment has been described in *Victims*, pp. 52, 121, and "Ex-Prosecutor Denies Politics Outran Justice," *Chicago Tribune*, 12/17/85, p. 1. See also *Hernandez* Brief, p. 41.

7 *Brian Dugan was arrested*: The details of Dugan's arrest, his subsequent statements, and the ensuing investigation have been recorded often. See, for example, *Cruz* II at 162 Ill. 2d at 331–42; *Hernandez* II at 18–23; *Victims*, pp. 99 fwd.

9 *seventeen men . . . sentenced to death and later . . . absolved*: The seventeen are Joseph Burrow, Perry Cobb, Rolando Cruz, Gary Gauger, Alex Hernandez, Madison Hobley, Stanley Howard, Verneal Jimerson, Ronald Jones, Carl Lawson, Steven Manning, Leroy Orange, Aaron Patterson, Anthony Porter, Steven Smith, Darby Tillis, and Dennis Williams. Links to a summary of each case appear on the Web site of Northwestern University Law School's Center on Wrongful Convictions, *http://www.law.northwestern.edu/depts/clinic/wrongful/exonerations/Illinois.htm*.

9 *Porter was released in February 1999*: Anthony Porter's story has been often told. See, e.g., D. Holt and S. Mills, "Double Murder Case Unravels," *Chicago Tribune* [North Sports Final Edition], 2/4/99,

p. 1, and the front page of the *Tribune* every day for the next week; Center on Wrongful Convictions; *http://www.illinoisdeathpenalty .com/porter.html.*

9 Chicago Tribune *published a relentless series*: K. Armstrong and S. Mills, "Death Row Justice Derailed," *Chicago Tribune*, 11/14/99, p. 1, began the *Tribune*'s noteworthy series. The remaining four parts ran the next four days. In point of fact, by the Commission's calculation, Illinois death sentences or the underlying convictions were reversed *more* than half the time. See Report of the Governor's Commission on Capital Punishment ["Report"], p. 204, n.29. The report is posted at *http://www.idoc.state.il.us/ccp.*

10 *the overall scorecard*: The scorecard numbers were those gathered by the Commission at the end of 2001, after the moratorium had been in place for two years. See Report, Technical Appendix, Section 2. At that time, there were approximately 15 additional defendants who had been convicted and sent to death row but who had not yet completed an initial appeal. Because the moratorium suspended executions, but not convictions, the numbers in all categories changed in ensuing years. In October 2002, the Illinois Department of Corrections issued a fact sheet that said 313 inmates had been admitted to the condemned unit since the death penalty was reestablished in Illinois in June 1977. "Of the 313 inmates, 123 had their sentence reversed, 2 had their sentence reversed and were discharged, 13 have died in prison, 12 have been executed in Illinois, 1 has been executed in Ohio, 1 has been pardoned and 1 has had the death sentence commuted." *http://www.idoc.state.il.us/subsections/ reports/news/condemnedunitstats.pdf.* Professor James Liebman of Columbia, whose empirical study of death penalty error rates has been highly publicized and hotly disputed (among other reasons, because he looked only to reversals, without regard to whether a death sentence was reimposed), has emphasized that Illinois' error rates are *lower* than the national average. See J. Liebman et al., "A Broken System: Error Rates in Capital Cases 1973–1995," posted at *http://justice.policy.net/jpreport/* and *http://justice.policy.net/jpreport/ liebman1.pdf* at iii.

10 *Governor Ryan found . . . death warrant . . . tormenting*: Ryan spoke often to reporters about the Kokoraleis execution and his reluctance

to repeat that experience. C. Falsani, "Present system makes moratorium 'a moral obligation,' gov says," *Chicago Sun-Times*, 3/15/02; E. Slater, "A Matter of Life and Death: Illinois Gov. George Ryan Backed Executions Until an Inmate's Fate Was in His Hands," *Los Angeles Times* [National Edition], 11/8/02, p. 1.

10  *system "fraught with error"*: For a summary of Governor Ryan's statement in declaring the moratorium and the generally positive reaction it garnered, see K. Armstrong and S. Mills, "Ryan: Until I Can Be Sure—Illinois Is First State to Suspend Death Penalty," *Chicago Tribune*, 2/1/00, p. 1.

12  *1978 . . . no federal death penalty*: The complicated history of the federal death penalty is discussed on the United States Department of Justice Web site. *http://www.usdoj.gov/dag/pubdoc/_dp_survey_final.pdf.*

14  *John Wayne Gacy was scheduled for execution*: Gacy's crimes are described in the opinion of the Illinois Supreme Court affirming Gacy's conviction and death sentence. *People v. Gacy*, 103 Ill. 2d 1; 468 N.E.2d 1171; 82 Ill. Dec. 391 (1984).

15  *Paul Simon . . . longtime foe of the death penalty*: Senator Simon described his own death-penalty conversion in his biography. P. Simon, *P.S.: The Autobiography of Paul Simon* (Bonus Books, 1998), pp. 73–74.

16  *By the time Ryan left office, at least fifty persons . . . convicted*: The so-called licenses-for-bribes scandal was a frequent topic of local coverage. For summaries, including a running count of those convicted, see E. Krol, "Secretary of State Hopeful Says Changes Are Needed," Chicagoland *Daily Herald*, 10/21/02; Illinois Campaign for Political Reform (ICPR), "Licenses for Bribes: The Roots of Corruption, Closer to the Top; State Employees Get Prison Time for Political Fundraising," January 2001, posted at *http://ilcampaign.org/issuebriefings/ib7.html* and the ICPR Web site, *http://ilcampaign.org/.*

16  *ex-chief of staff and Ryan's political campaign fund . . . were convicted in March 2003*: M. O'Connor, "Jury Convicts Fawell, Ryan Campaign of Fraud," *Chicago Tribune*, 3/20/03, p. 1. The article places at fifty-five the number of persons convicted in connection with the federal investigation of Ryan's Secretary of State's office.

17 *Ryan was a pharmacist*: Biographies of George Ryan appear at the Web site of the Illinois Blue Book, 2000 Millennium Edition, pp. 20–21, *http://www.cyberdriveillinois.com/bb/sec1_1_34.pdf*, and 2001–2002 Edition, *http://www.sos.state.il.us/publications/02bluebook/portraits_bios/georgehryan.pdf*.

20 *report by Raymond Paternoster*: Paternoster's study appears at *http://www.urhome.umd.edu/newsdesk/pdf/exec.pdf*. Final report: *http://www.urhome.umd.edu/newsdesk/pdf/finalrep.pdf*. The Maryland debate is summarized often; e.g., *http://www.quixote.org/ej/states/maryland/*.

20 *Indiana established . . . Commission*: Regarding the Indiana study, see Report, p. 198 and pp. 204–5, n.35, and the study itself, "The Application of Indiana's Capital Sentencing Law: Findings of Indiana Criminal Law Study Commission," available from the Indiana Criminal Justice Institute, One North Capitol, Suite 1000, Indianapolis, IN 46204-2038 [hereafter "Indiana Report"].

21 *committee appointed by the Pennsylvania Supreme Court*: A. Liptak, "Suspension of Executions Is Urged for Pennsylvania," *New York Times* [National Edition], 3/5/03, p. A15.

21 *constitutional right to have that jury . . . decide*: The sentencing scheme in Arizona, which allowed a judge to impose a death sentence after a jury verdict, was invalidated in *Ring v. Arizona*, 536 U.S. 584 (2002). The decision seemingly also rendered unconstitutional the systems in Idaho, Nebraska, and Colorado and brought into question the sentencing statutes in Montana, Florida, Alabama, Indiana, and Delaware. Whether *Ring* applies retroactively to the death sentences previously pronounced under those systems has not yet been decided.

21 *federal capital punishment statute is unconstitutional*: Judge William Sessions III declared the federal capital statute unconstitutional on 9/24/02 in *United States v. Fell*, 217 F. Supp. 2d 469 (D.Vt. 2002). For press accounts, see, e.g., *http://www.usatoday.com/news/nation/2002-09-24-death-penalty-unconstitutional_x.htm*.

21 *execution of the mentally retarded is unconstitutional*: The U.S. Supreme Court prohibited death sentences for the mentally retarded in *Atkins v. Virginia*, 536 U.S. 304 (2002).

21 *four justices . . . executing murderers . . . under eighteen . . . cruel and un-*

*usual*: In *In Re Stanford, 537 U.S.–,* 123 S.Ct. 715, 71 U.S.L.W. 3416 (No. 10009, 10/21/02), Justices Stevens, Breyer, Ginsburg, and Souter dissented from the Court's decision not to review the question of whether execution of a person under eighteen was unconstitutional, in light of *Atkins*. Because the case was on collateral review—i.e., not on the direct chain of appeal from the original judgment—four votes could not bring the matter before the Court. But four votes will be sufficient when the question is presented on direct review of the conviction and death sentence of another defendant. Even among the thirty-eight states that permit capital punishment, twenty-one, including Illinois, plus the federal government and the military, prohibit the execution of juveniles under seventeen. See *http://www.deathpenaltyinfo.org/article.php? did-205&scid-27*.

21  *nudged the door wider*: *Miller-El v. Cockrell*, No. 01-7662 (decided 2/25/03).

21  *raised the bar for a defense lawyer's duty*: *Wiggins v. Smith*, No. 02-311 (decided 6/26/03). The New York Court of Appeals also overturned that state's first death sentence. *People v. Harris*, 98 N.Y. 2d 452, 779 N.E.2d 705, 749 N.Y.S. 2d 766 (2002); *http://www.courts.state.ny.us/ctapps/decisions/jul02.htm*.

22  *each state . . . imposed death for a long list of felonies*: For death penalty history, see, e.g., Justice Marshall's concurrence in *Furman v. Georgia*, 408 U.S. 238, 336–42 (1972); "Background and Developments" in *The Death Penalty in America: Current Controversies*, Hugo Adam Bedau, ed. (Oxford University Press, 1997) [hereafter "*The Death Penalty in America*"], pp. 3–25; N. Levi, "Veil of Secrecy: Public Executions," 55 *Federal Communications Law Journal* 131 (2002), pp. 131–41.

22  *1966 . . . majority . . . opposed capital punishment*: In 1966, Gallup reported that 47 percent of Americans were against the death penalty, while 42 percent were for it. The numbers in favor soon climbed, especially after the decision in *Furman*. See J. Jones, "The Death Penalty," posted on the Gallup Organization's Web site, *http://www.gallup.com/poll/analysis/ia020830.asp*, for a detailed summary of Gallup's findings about public opinion on the death penalty over the years.

22  *Furman v. Georgia*: 408 U.S. 238 (1972).

23  *imposing death, was constitutional after all*: *Gregg v. Georgia*, 428 U.S. 153 (1976) held that the death penalty is not unconstitutional in every instance in which it is applied.

23  *DNA . . . showed . . . innocent people . . . convicted*: *The New York Times* puts the number of recent DNA exonerations as 123. T. Simon, "Freedom Row," *The New York Times Magazine*, 1/25/03, p. 32.

23  *Death Penalty Information Center counted 108 persons*: Summaries of all innocence cases are posted at the Death Penalty Information Center's Web site at *http://www.deathpenaltyinfo.org/innoc.html*.

23  *dozens of additional cases*: The Death Penalty Information Center catalogs cases of probable and possible innocence, in which there has not been a legal outcome impugning the original judgment, at *http://www.deathpenaltyinfo.org/article.php.scid-6&did-111#Released*.

23  *only 49 percent of Americans favored capital punishment*: Gallup reported that only 52 percent of Americans believe that the death penalty is imposed fairly, while 40 percent do not. Gallup News Service, 5/20/02. ABCnews.com 1/24/03 featured the poll results that showed that less than half of Americans support the death penalty when life in prison is offered as an alternative. Without that choice, 64 percent said they favored the death penalty. All of these results, and many others, appear at *http://www.deathpenaltyinfo.org/Polls.html*.

25  *Commission . . . assembled to represent diverse viewpoints and experience*: The Members of the Commission are described at Report at v.

28  *confessions are obtained in roughly 40 percent of arrests*: Professor Paul Cassell of the University of Utah is among those who have made the most comprehensive efforts to determine U.S. confession rates, as part of his controversial studies aimed at proving that the U.S. Supreme Court's ruling in *Miranda v. Arizona*, 384 U.S. 435 (1966), has impeded law enforcement. See, e.g., P. Cassell, "*Miranda's* Social Costs: An Empirical Reassessment," *90 Northwestern University Law Review* 387 (1996), and a related piece Cassell published on the Web site of the National Center for Policy Analysis, "Handcuffing the Cops: Miranda's Harmful Effects on Law Enforcement," posted at *http://www.ncpa.org/studies/s218/s218a.html*, and his confession data at *http://www.ncpa.org/studies/s218/s218a.html#confession*.

28 *"All I did was hold that little girl down"*: To be precise, the "I held her down" statement was introduced in Alex's second and third trials as an overheard remark. It was testified to by Marquez in paraphrase when Alex was first tried in 1985. See *People v. Hernandez*, 121 Ill. 2d 293, 302, 521 N.E.2d 25, 117 Ill. Dec. 914 (1988). The Marquez encounter and related evidence is described in our brief, pp. 8–10, 15–16, 75–83, and in *Hernandez* I, 121 Ill. 2d at 303, *Hernandez* II, pp. 6–8.

29 *Alex's IQ was low*: although prosecution experts found Alex's IQ higher, an IQ of 73, under new legislation passed in Illinios in May 2003, would render a defendant presumptively ineligible for the death penalty. See C. Parsons and R. Long, "Death Penalty Reform Goes to Blagojevich," *Chicago Tribune* [Final Edition], 5/30/03, p. 1.

30 *Gary Gauger*: Gauger's case, like Alex's, was reversed in an unpublished decision of the Illinois Appellate Court Second District, this one on 3/8/96. *People v. Gauger*, 277 Ill.App.3d 1114, 698 N.E.2d 724. See also 168 Ill. 2d 606, 671 N.E.2d 736, 219 Ill. Dec. 569 (1996). In 1997, James Schneider and Randall E. Miller, members of the Outlaws motorcycle gang, were indicted in federal court in Milwaukee for racketeering charges that included killing the Gaugers. Schneider pled guilty in 1998. Audiotaped admissions by Miller about his role in the murders were played at his trial in 2000, in which he was convicted. See "Motorcycle Gang Member Detailed Illinois Murders," *Beloit Daily News*, 3/10/99, posted at *http://www.beloitdailynews.com/399/1wis10.htm* and *http://www.law.northwestern.edu/depts/clinic/wrongful/exonerations/Gaugerchart.pdf.*

30 *Ronald Jones*: Ronald Jones's conviction was originally affirmed by the Illinois Supreme Court, *People v. Jones*, 156 Ill. 2d 225, 620 N.E.2d 325 (1994), and subsequently vacated. 1997 WL 1113760. His exoneration was recounted in the pages of the *Chicago Tribune* on 5/18/99 and in *The New York Times* the next day. Despite the DNA corroboration for Jones's account of being beaten, there is no record of disciplinary action regarding the two detectives who interrogated Jones.

31 *Cruz case . . . no confession*: Thomas Vosburgh and Dennis Kurzawa were indicted in sealed indictments returned in December 1996.

Included were charges for perjury for testifying to the vision statement. Thomas Knight was charged with knowingly presenting false evidence to the grand jury. See *Victims*, pp. 284–85; A. Barnum and T. Gregory, "Impending Indictments in Cruz Scandal Rock DuPage," *Chicago Tribune* [DuPage Sports Final], 12/10/96, p. 1; T. Gregory, "DuPage Judge Is Target in Cruz Case," *Chicago Tribune*, 12/11/96.

31 *forgotten about the statement*: The "vision statement" is described in *Cruz I*, 121 Ill. 2d at 324, and *Cruz II*, 162 Ill. 2d at 322. See also *Victims*, pp. 70–71.

31 *Central Park jogger case*: S. Maull, "Judge Throws Out Convictions in Central Park Jogger Case," Associated Press, 12/20/02, posted at *http://www.post-gazette.com/nation/20021220apjoggercasenat2p2.asp*. As in *Cruz* and *Hernandez*, the New York City police continue to insist they got the right men. See, e.g., *http://www.nyc.gov/html/nypd/ html/dcpi/jogger_case_panel.html*.

31 *Porter . . . falsely identified*: See *People v. Porter*, 111 Ill. 2d 386, 391–93, 489 N.E.2d 1329, 95 Ill. Dec. 465 (1986), for the Illinois Supreme Court's confident account of Porter's identification.

31 *Buckley . . . identified*: See *Victims*, p. 86, for a description of the eyewitness testimony regarding Buckley.

31 *mistaken identification . . . leading cause of wrongful convictions*: T. Simon, "Freedom Row," *The New York Times Magazine*, 1/25/03, p. 32, states that incorrect eyewitness identifications remain the largest reason for wrongful convictions nationwide. See also C. R. Huff, "Wrongful Conviction: Causes and Public Policy Issues," *Criminal Justice*, Spring 2003, pp. 15–16. The Commission found two articles about eyewitness testimony especially significant: G. Wells, "Eyewitness Identification Procedures: Recommendations for Lineups and Photospreads," *Law and Human Behavior*, Vol. 22, No. 6, 1998, and "Eyewitness Identification: A Guide for Law Enforcement," prepared by the Technical Working Group for Eyewitness Evidence sponsored by the National Institute of Justice, U.S. Department of Justice, October 1999.

32 *"caution and great care"*: Instruction 3.13, "Pattern Criminal Federal Jury Instructions for the Seventh Circuit," 1998, posted at

*http://www.ca7.uscourts.gov/Rules/pjury.pdf*, is an example of an instruction containing the traditional warning to jurors to take accomplice testimony with "caution and great care."

32 *Burrows . . . Jimerson . . . Williams*: See *People v. Joseph Burrows*, 148 Ill. 2d 196, 592 N.E.2d 997 (1992), and 172 Ill. 2d 169, 665 N.E.2d 1319 (1996) (affirming order for new trial) and Northwestern's Center on Wrongful Convictions summary of the case at *http://www.law.northwestern.edu/depts/clinic/wrongful/exonerations/Burrows Chart.pdf*; *People v. Jimerson*, 166 Ill. 2d 211, 652 N.E.2d 278 (1995), and R. Warden's lengthy chronology of the case popularly known as the Ford Heights Four, posted at *http://www.illinoisdeathpenalty .com/chron.doc*.

33 *juries fail in their enshrined role*: For a brief recounting of the evolution of the jury as bulwark against governmental abuse, see my short piece about the trial of William Penn, "Order in the Court," *The New York Times Magazine*, 4/18/99, p. 25.

33 *avoid the death penalty . . . by pleading guilty*: For example, "The Federal Death Penalty System: A Statistical Survey" published by the U.S. Department of Justice, 9/12/00, *http://www.usdoj.gov/dag/pub doc/dpsurvey.html*, DoJ's survey of federal death penalty cases from 1995 to 2000, showed that of 108 cases approved for capital prosecution that had proceeded through trial, 51 defendants had avoided death by pleading guilty. Forty-one had gone to trial, with 21 receiving death sentences. *http://www.usdoj.gov/dag/pubdoc/_table_ set_i_corrected.pdf*.

33 *an innocent person . . . might plead*: Such a plea is constitutional. *North Carolina v. Alford*, 400 U.S. 25 (1970). While the Commission contemplated recommending a ban on plea negotiations once the state had decided to seek death, both defense lawyers and prosecutors counseled against this. See Report, p. 124.

34 *any person who . . . will refuse*: *Witherspoon v. Illinois*, 391 U.S. 510 (1968), held that mere disagreement with the death penalty does not disqualify a juror. Although *Witherspoon* essentially broadened, rather than narrowed, the potential venire in a capital case, it nonetheless contains language allowing disqualification of jurors who state that they will automatically vote against the death penalty, no matter what the trial evidence shows; see *Witherspoon*,

391 U.S. at 513–14n.5, 515–16n.9, 521–22n.20, the point upon which many subsequent courts have cited it. See, e.g., *Lockhart v. McCree*, 476 U.S. 162, 167n.1 (1986); *People v. Harris*, 98 N.Y.2d at 477.

34 *resulting jury pool is more conviction-prone*: *Witherspoon*, *McCree*, and *Harris*, discussed in the preceding note, all dismissed the studies purporting to show that juries without death penalty objectors were more likely to convict. *Witherspoon*, 391 U.S. at 516–17 ("data . . . are too fragmentary and tentative"); *McCree*, 476 U.S. at 171 ("We have serious doubts about the value of these studies in predicting the behavior of actual jurors"); *Harris*, 98 N.Y.2d at 479n.8. More to the point, *McCree* held flatly that even if the studies were correct, a conviction-prone jury does not violate the Constitution, since the state has a legitimate interest in seating a jury that will follow the law. 476 U.S. at 176–84.

34 *one in every fifty convictions . . . resulted in a capital sentence*: Analysis of the frequency of death sentences in Illinois is set forth at the Report, at 197, 204n.28 and in Technical Appendix, Section 1.

34 *Wyoming . . . has the highest death-sentencing rate*: Liebman collected per capita death-sentencing rates for thirty-four of the thirty-eight states that impose the death penalty, which showed Wyoming to be the national leader at nearly 6 percent of all homicides. *http://jus tice.policy.net/jpreport/section7.html#a* and *http://justice.policy.net/jpre port/figure17.html*. The same study showed that Illinois' proportion of death sentences per first-degree homicides is comparable to the nation as a whole. Liebman reports that for the thirty-four capital-sentencing states, an average of 14.9 death sentences were imposed for every 1,000 homicides during the study period, of 1973–95, meaning roughly 1.5 percent: *http://justice.policy.net/jpreport/ section7.html#a*. Liebman's figures, however, consider "homicides," rather than the narrower universe of first-degree murders Radelet and Pierce studied. According to Liebman's figures, Illinois averaged 9.89 death sentences per 1,000 homicides, roughly 1 percent, less than the national average. *http://justice.policy.net/jpreport/fig ure17.html* and *http://justice.policy.net/jpreport/illinois.pdf*.

34 *death . . . not . . . automatic punishment for first-degree murder*: In *Woodson v. North Carolina*, 428 U.S. 280 (1976), the Supreme Court de-

clared unconstitutional a North Carolina statute that imposed death for all first-degree murders, holding that the Eighth Amendment's ban on cruel and unusual punishment requires contemplation of the circumstances of a particular crime and the character of a defendant before death may be imposed.

34  *"the worst of the worst"*: "The death penalty's reserved for the worst of the worst. And I think from the evidence that all of you are aware of over the last month or so these folks qualify," said Commonwealth Attorney Paul Ebert of Prince William County about the Beltway Sniper suspects. *http://www.cnn.com/2002/US/11/07/sniper.case/*. See *Gregg v. Georgia*, 428 U.S. at 198 (there should be a meaningful basis for distinguishing the few cases in which the death penalty is imposed from the many where it is not).

35  *intended to be a burglary, committed by . . . Hispanics*: See *Victims*, pp. 26–27, for an account of the Spanish-surnamed burglar and at 120 for quotations from the lead detective, John Sam, about the theory that the crime was committed by a gang of Hispanic burglars.

35  *sought an outside legal opinion*: R. Karwath and J. Sjostrom, "Burris Holds Firm on Nicarico Case," *Chicago Tribune* [DuPage Sports Final Edition], 3/7/92, p. 5, reported the remarks of Anton Valukas, who'd been hired to review the case.

35  *Sam . . . had quit*: Sam's resignation was news. See "Resignations Cast Doubts on Handling of Nicarico Case," *Chicago Tribune*, 12/15/85, p. 1, and *Victims*, pp. 62–64.

35  *James Teal*: Teal's doubts are recounted at *Victims*, pp. 60–62 and 127–28. After Hernandez's second conviction, the former police chief wrote a letter to the sentencing judge in Hernandez's behalf expressing the view that Alex was innocent. *Hernandez* Brief, p. 40.

35  *Marquez . . . disavowed his testimony*: Marquez's recantations are described in the *Hernandez* Brief, p. 29n.12.

35  *Marquez evidence through a police officer*: The *Hernandez* Brief, p. 9, describes the officer's testimony with citations to the court record.

36  *"impossible to determine"*: The *Hernandez* Brief, pp. 26–28, quotes Judge Nelligan's remarks from the trial record and his summary of the officer's testimony.

36  *"the one statement that tied this Defendant"*: This quote comes from

Judge Nelligan's remarks at Alex's sentencing, set out in the *Hernandez* Brief, p. 26–28.

37 any *rational jury*: *Jackson v. Virginia*, 443 U.S. 307, 319 (1979), sets forth the standard for review of a jury's verdict. In *Hernandez* II, p. 23, the Court followed the familiar practice of quoting *Jackson* and underlining "*any*," so the verdict cannot be disturbed if "*any* rational trier of fact" could have reached the same conclusion. See *People v. Collins*, 116 Ill. 2d 237, 261 (1985).

37 *Nelligan . . . regarded the meaning . . . as "impossible to determine"*: In Alex's appeal, we maintained that the Marquez statement, as testified to by the officer, was so devoid of context as to be meaningless, and therefore improperly received in evidence. The Appellate Court declined to address the issue, finding that the trial lawyers had failed to offer a timely objection, making the question unreviewable on appeal. See *Hernandez* II, pp. 16–17. During argument, the court had appeared so interested in the issue that afterwards both parties made supplemental filings on the law.

37 *Matt Tanner and Leslie Suson, and I appeared before the Illinois Appellate Court*: See *Victims*, p. 261, for an account of the oral argument in *Hernandez* II.

38 *appellate courts refuse to . . . "retry his case"*: Thus in reviewing the evidence of Alex's guilt, the Court in *Hernandez* II stated, "It is not the province of this court . . . to retry the defendant," meaning, in short, "It's not up to us to decide if he's actually guilty."

38 *Porter's lawyers . . . developed . . . proof that . . . Simon*: Porter's lawyers' contentions regarding Alstory Simon were summarized by the Illinois Supreme Court: "The evidence pointed to is the proposed testimony of several persons which could have suggested Alstory Simon, rather than defendant, killed Hillard and Green. The evidence, summarized below, is stated in affidavits and recorded sworn oral statements filed in support of defendant's post-conviction petition. Joyce Haywood would have testified that the victims had walked to the park with Alstory Simon and his girlfriend, Inez Johnson. The victims' mothers and Christina Green, Marilyn Green's sister, would have corroborated the point. Ricky Young could have testified that Hillard had been selling drugs for Simon and that a dispute existed between Simon and Hillard over money.

Roy Davis, Hillard's brother, would have stated, in contrast, that no animosity existed between defendant and Hillard, who were members of the same street gang. Finally, Joyce Haywood would have revealed further that Simon had threatened her when she had asked about what had happened in the park." *People v. Porter*, 164 Ill. 2d 400, 403–4, 647 N.E.2d 972, 207 Ill. Dec. 479 (1995). See also *Porter v. Warden*, No. 95 C 4111 (United States District Court for the Northern District of Illinois, 4/3/96); *Porter v. Gramley*, 112 F.3d 1308 (7th Cir. 1997); *People v. Porter*, 111 Ill. 2d 386, 489 N.E.2d 1329, 95 Ill. Dec. 465 (1986). No court ever found Porter's evidence of innocence compelling. Thus the Seventh Circuit said in Porter's last *habeas corpus* appeal: "[T]he affidavits *and* statements that Porter has submitted are far from convincing, especially when weighed against the direct, eyewitness testimony implicating Porter. Much of the evidence suggesting that someone other than Porter committed the murders, for example, is second- and third-hand in nature, and the first-hand information (such as the affidavit stating that victim Jerry Hillard was arguing in the park that night with someone other than Porter) can only be considered weak circumstantial evidence of Porter's innocence." *Porter v. Gramley*, 122 F.3d 351, 353 (7th Cir, 1997).

39 *"Death is different"*: The saying is a paraphrase of Justice Stewart's remark in *Woodson v. North Carolina*, 428 U.S. 280, 303–4 (1976), where he stated that "death is a punishment different from all other sanctions in kind rather than degree."

39 *four . . . persons . . . ultimately exonerated*: For an article tracking what happened to those whose lives *Furman* spared, see J. Marquart and J. Sorensen, "A National Study of *Furman*-Commuted Prisoners: Assessing the Threat to Society from Capital Offenders," reprinted in *The Death Penalty in America*, p. 164.

39 *bravest advocates of capital punishment*: William Kunkle, the former First Assistant State's Attorney in Chicago, is one such death penalty proponent willing to take this position.

42 *murder rate in . . . United States . . . four times . . . European Union*: The murder rates cited come from a document on the Web site of the British Home Office, G. Barclay, C. Tavares, A. Siddique, "International Comparisons of Criminal Justice Statistics 1999," Home

Office Bulletin, Issue 6/01, May 2001, posted at *http://www.home office.gov.uk/rds/pdfs/hosb601.pdf*. Other data is collected at *http:// www.angelfire.com/rnb/y/homicide.htm#murd*.

42 *not fair that Europeans judge us*: Tending to prove that Europeans get as angry as Americans in the face of crime is the French election of 2002, when a rise in immigrants' crimes was the cited reason that Lionel Jospin of the Socialists, the traditional opponents of the ruling Gaulists, didn't make the runoffs for French President. Instead, Jospin was outpolled by Jean-Marie Le Pen, who probably would have been comfortable with a klaxon and bedsheet in the American South of the 1930s. See, for example, "Shock Success for French Far Right," *http://news.bbc.co.uk/1/hi/world/europe/ 1942612.stm*.

43 *prosecutors emphasized two different shoeprints*: The shoeprint incident, with transcript quotations and citations, is set out at pp. 43–46 of the *Hernandez* Brief. See *Victims*, pp. 193–94, detailing how the prosecutors had used the same prints and the same theories to send Cruz to death row.

44 *far smaller woman's size*: A woman's size-six shoe corresponds to a man's four or four and a half, a size I've yet to see on the shelf of any men's store. See *http://onlineconversion.com/womens_clothing. htm*; *http://funkefeet.com/funk-shoeSize.html*. In *Victims*, Frisbee and Garrett say that Detective John Sam had been assured in 1983 that these shoeprints had been made by friends of Jeanine's sister who had run around the house looking for the little girl in the immediate aftermath of her disappearance (*Victims*, p. 34). The size of the prints, and the women's tread design positively identified on one of them, obviously fortifies that explanation.

44 *first . . . trial . . . reversed*: The quotation on the prosecutors' deliberate misuse of evidence comes from *People v. Cruz*, 121 Ill. 2d 293, 333, 521, N.E.2d 18 (1988). See also *People v. Hernandez*, 521 N.E.2d 25.

44 *more inadmissible proof*: *Cruz* II, 162 Ill. 2d at 355–58, details the prosecutors' impeachment of Irma Rodriquez. "[W]e cannot but conclude that the motivation . . . was improper," the Court said. *Id.* at 363.

45 *jailhouse witnesses . . . testify they had no deal*: *Cruz* II, 162 Ill. 2d at

328, describes how Robert Turner, a death row informant who'd been a witness against Cruz, testified that Robert Kilander, one of the Cruz trial prosecutors, never said anything to Turner about Kilander's providing favorable testimony for him. Kilander later testified when Turner was resentenced and acknowledged that before getting on the stand against Cruz, Turner wanted to be certain Kilander would testify, 162 Ill. 2d at 332, which, the Court said, "clearly impugns" Turner's testimony. *Hernandez* I, 121 Ill. 2d at 308, recounts an incident at the first Hernandez trial in which Tom Knight, the original prosecutor of these cases, called an Assistant State's Attorney from a neighboring county as a witness to testify that Marquez received no preferential treatment and that Knight never spoke to the Assistant about that. The neighboring prosecutor was then impeached with the transcript of Marquez's sentencing, which showed that Knight had in fact requested leniency for Marquez. See also *Victims*, p. 78.

45 *officer said . . . he'd actually been in Florida*: See *Victims*, pp. 269–70; M. Possley, "Cruz's Legal Defense Team Worked for Free, But Not for Nothing—Single Date Cracks the Code of Freedom," *Chicago Tribune*, 11/6/95, p. 1.

45 *indictment of seven men*: See *Victims*, pp. 284–85; A. Barnum, T. Gregory, "Impending Indictments in Cruz Scandal Rock DuPage," *Chicago Tribune* [DuPage Sports Final], 12/10/96, p. 1; T. Gregory, "DuPage Judge Is Target in Cruz Case," *Chicago Tribune*, 12/11/96.

45 *law enforcement officers . . . acquitted*: M. Possley and T. Gregory, "DuPage 5 Win Acquittal," *Chicago Tribune*, 6/5/99.

45 *multimillion-dollar settlement*: See, e.g., J. Chase, "Angry DuPage Settles Cruz Suits—3 Former Defendants to Split $3.5 Million," *Chicago Tribune* [Chicago Sports Final, N Edition], 9/27/00, p. 1; "Acquitted Ill. Men Win Settlement" at *http://www.crimelynx.com/cruz.html*.

46 *that DNA establishes Dugan's role with "scientific certainty"*: Birkett, who ran for Illinois Attorney General and was chastised for his alleged part in the Cruz/Hernandez case during the campaign, did not disclose the new DNA results concerning Dugan until after he had lost the election. See S. Mills and C. Parsons, "Birkett Clings to Cruz Link in Killing," *Chicago Tribune* [North Sports Final Edi-

tion], 11/15/02, p. 1. See also "Acquitted Ill. Men Win Settlement" at *http://www.crimelynx.com/cruz.html* (" 'It is morally repugnant to give money to someone we think may have committed this crime,' Birkett said").

46 *attempted to strip Ronald Mehling of his position as Presiding Judge*: *Victims*, p. 278; see also A. Barnum, "High Profile Case Judge to Retire," *Chicago Tribune*, 6/20/02.

46 *Robert Kilander . . . now the Chief Judge*: A. Barnum, "Kilander Voted County's Chief Judge," *Chicago Tribune*, 1/17/01.

48 *U.S. Supreme Court had ruled . . . unconstitutional . . . statement of . . . impact*: *Booth v. Maryland*, 482 U.S. 496 (1987) ruled victim impact testimony unconstitutional in a capital sentencing hearing.

49 *Court . . . reversed itself*: In *Payne v. Tennessee*, 501 U.S. 808 (1991), the Court explicitly overruled *Booth* and concluded that victim impact testimony could permissibly contribute to an assessment of a defendant's blameworthiness by helping measure the harm of his crime.

49 *Now . . . victims have a statutory right . . . to be heard*: Chapter 725, Act 120, of the Illinois Compiled Statutes (720 ILCS 120/1) is the Rights of Crime Victims and Witnesses Act. Section 120/4(4) gives victims the right to address the court at sentencing. Other rights protected by the statute include notification of court proceedings, a right to be present or to have a representative present in court, and the right of restitution.

49 *"[M]y 10 year-old daughter"*: Citations to Mrs. Larson's testimony are from the transcript of the 12/13/00 Commission session conducted in Springfield, Illinois.

50 *Laura Tucker*: Ms. Tucker appeared before the Commission in Chicago on 8/2/00.

50 *Apprendi v. New Jersey*: 530 U.S. 466 (2000).

51 *less than half of one percent had actually been executed*: In Illinois, for example, before the moratorium roughly 285 persons had been sentenced to death but only 12 executed. This is not an anomalous result. In his national study, Professor Liebman of Columbia found that as of 1995, across the country more than 5,700 death sentences had been imposed since *Furman*, but only 313 had been carried out. *http://justice.policy.net/jpreport/section7.html#a*.

52 *"I thought I would feel satisfied"*: Jay Stratton is quoted in M. Pearl,

"Dante and the Death Penalty," *Legal Affairs*, January–February 2003, p. 38.

52 *survivors only experience more emotional turbulence*: J. Diaz, *The Execution of a Serial Killer* (Poncha Press 2003), p. 130, a fine narrative describing a scholar's reaction to being a witness at an execution, deals briefly with the slight literature of victims' post-execution reactions. See also R. J. Lifton, G. Mitchell, *Who Owns Death?: Capital Punishment, the American Conscience, and the End of Executions* (HarperCollins, 2002), pp. 197–212. Some murder survivors, such as those in Murder Victims' Families for Reconciliation, insist forthrightly, "Executions are not what will help us heal." See, generally, Murder Victims' Families for Reconciliation Web site, *http://www.mvfr.org/homepage.html*.

52 *told reporters . . . experienced a sense of relief*: *http://www.cnn.com/ 2001/LAW/06/11/victims.reax/* describes the reported reaction of many of the survivors who witnessed McVeigh's execution.

53 *critics may label the survivors' desire for death "retribution"*: For an outstanding discussion of retribution, revenge, and other questions regarding victims in particular and capital punishment in general, see A. Sarat, *When the State Kills* (Princeton University Press, 2001), pp. 33–59.

53 *Ackerman family . . . Nicaricos*: A. Barnum, "Melissa's Killer Pleads Guilty, Gets Life," *Chicago Tribune* [National Edition], 11/20/85, Section C, p. 1, describes Mr. Ackerman's reaction to the plea deal. The Nicaricos' doggedness about the case and their disappointment with Hernandez's eighty-year sentence, rather than death, is recorded at J. Sjostrom, "Hernandez Gets 80-Year Term in Nicarico Death," *Chicago Tribune* [DuPage Sports Final], p. 1. See another article quoted without attribution at *http://www.littlest angels.net/Stories229.html*.

55 *American law has exalted the jury's role in capital matters*: The Supreme Court's decision in June 2002, *Ring v. Arizona*, 536 U.S. 584, effectively granted to every defendant the right to have his fate decided by a jury. That was already the prevailing practice in all but nine states that impose the death penalty. The reason for the jury's unique prominence in making capital decisions is probably best expressed in the dissent of Justice Stevens in *Spaziano v.*

*Florida*, 468 U.S. 447, 489–90 (1984), where he said, "If the prosecutor cannot convince a jury that the defendant deserves to die, there is an unjustifiable risk that imposition of that punishment will not reflect the community's sense of the defendant's 'moral guilt.' "

56 *better job in providing compassionate services*: Report, pp. 192–94, and Technical Appendix, Sections 1B & C, detail issues related to survivors.

57 *"only reason to be for it"*: The third presidential debate took place on 10/17/00 at Washington University in St. Louis.

58 *has a murder rate well above the national average*: As of March of this year, Texas had executed 299 of the 834 persons put to death in the United States since *Gregg* reauthorized capital punishment. See P. Kilborn, "Prominent Ex-Judges and Prosecutors Lead Fight Against Milestone Execution Today in Texas," *The New York Times* [National Edition], 3/12/03, at A16. A summary of the FBI's Uniform Crime Reports and the murder rates in all the states from 1995 to 2001 is posted on the Death Penalty Information Web site at *http://www.deathpenaltyinfo.org/murderrates.html*. As an aside, stereotypes notwithstanding, Texas did not death-sentence more often than average, condemning 15.33 defendants per 1,000 homicides. But Texas *executes* a far higher percentage of those on death row than the national norms, suggesting that whatever issues exist in Texas have to do with the limitations the state has imposed on judicial review. See Liebman, *http://justice.policy.net/jpreport/figure 18.html* and *http://justice.policy.net/jpreport/texas.pdf*. See also National Center for Policy Analysis, "Capital Punishment Rates in Death Penalty States," 2/15/02, posted at *http://www.ncpa.org/iss/cri/2002/pd021502f.html*, and another of Liebman's reports, James S. Liebman et al., "A Broken System, Part II: Why There Is So Much Error in Capital Cases, and What Can Be Done About It," University of Columbia Law School, February 2002, posted at *http://www.law.columbia.edu/brokensystem2/index2.html*. Notably, more than half of Texas' 254 counties imposed no death sentences during Liebman's study period, but Harris County, whose seat is Houston, has sent more persons to death row than any other county in America.

58 *consolidated murder rate in states without the death penalty ... consistently lower*: Regarding state cross-comparisons, see *http://www.death penaltyinfo.org/DeterMRates. html*; *The New York Times*, 9/22/00, p. 1. Various studies and statistics regarding deterrence are summarized on the outstanding Web site of the Death Penalty Information Center at *http://www.deathpenaltyinfo.org/deter.html* - STUDIES.

58 *brutalization effect ... proof*: See for example, W. Bailey, "Deterrence, Brutalization, and the Death Penalty: Another Examination of Oklahoma's Return to Capital Punishment," 36 *Criminology*, pp. 711–33 (1998), for a disciplined examination of both brutalization and deterrence in Oklahoma's homicide statistics.

58 *murder rates drop ... since 1993*: See J. Fox and M. Zawitz, "Homicide Trends in the United States," United States Department of Justice, Bureau of Justice Statistics, *http://www.ojp.usdoj.gov/bjs/homicide/homtrnd.htm*.

59 *clearest deterrent effect from executions*: Without executions, the death penalty would come to be perceived as an empty threat. The certainty of punishment is key to its effectiveness, according to deterrence theory. W. Bailey and R. Peterson, "Murder, Capital Punishment and Deterrence: A Review of the Literature," in *The Death Penalty in America*, p. 140. See the sources discussed in the next several notes for elaboration, including H. Dezhbakhsh et al., "Does Capital Punishment Have a Deterrent Effect? New Evidence from Post Moratorium Panel Data," January 2001, pp. 20–21, which can be downloaded at *http://userwww.service.emory.edu/~cozden/dezhbakhsh_01_cover.html* [hereafter "Dezhbakhsh"]. Dezhbakhsh, pp. 22–23, found a deterrent effect in arrests, sentencings, and executions, but claimed their most robust results were in connection with executions. The claim that arrests produce a deterrent effect, given that the vast majority of arrests do not result in a death sentence, hardly supports capital punishment, as opposed to locking up bad guys.

59 *"studies ... yielded ... fairly consistent pattern of non-deterrence"*: W. Bailey & R. Peterson, "Murder, Capital Punishment and Deterrence," 50 *Journal of Social Issues*, p. 53, Summer 1994.

59 *Eighty percent said it did not*: M. Radelet and R. Akers, "Deterrence

and the Death Penalty: The Views of the Experts," 87 *Journal of Criminal Law and Criminology* 1, Fall 1996.

59 *police chiefs . . . inaccurate to say . . . death penalty . . . reduces . . . homicides*: See R. Dieter, "On the Front Line: Law Enforcement Views on the Death Penalty," posted at *http://www.deathpenaltyinfo.org/dpic.ro3.html*, which presents the results of the Hart poll.

59 *academic support for deterrence . . . from free-market economists*: E.g., Ehrlich, "The Deterrent Effect of Capital Punishment," 65 *The American Economic Review*, pp. 397–417 (1975); H. Dezhbakhsh passim.

60 *Ehrlich's results . . . U.S. Supreme Court . . . reauthorize capital punishment*: See *Gregg v. Georgia* for the Court's discussion of deterrence. The Court appeared less than fully persuaded, remarking: "Statistical attempts to evaluate the worth of the death penalty as a deterrent to crimes by potential offenders have occasioned a great deal of debate. The results simply have been inconclusive." 428 U.S. at 184–85. Notwithstanding that judgment, the Court ruled that legislators were within constitutional bounds in finding deterrence a justification for the death penalty.

60 *Ehrlich and his followers have been stingingly criticized*: Peck, "The Deterrent Effect of Capital Punishment: Ehrlich and His Critics," 85 *Yale L. J.* 359 (1976); Baldus & Cole, "A Comparison of the Work of Thorsten Sellin and Isaac Ehrlich on the Deterrent Effect of Capital Punishment," 85 *Yale L. J.* 170 (1975); Bowers & Pierce, "The Illusion of Deterrence in Isaac Ehrlich's Research on Capital Punishment," 85 *Yale L. J.* 187 (1975); W. Bailey and R. Peterson, "Murder, Capital Punishment and Deterrence: A Review of the Literature," in *The Death Penalty in America*, pp. 135–61.

60 *A 2001 paper . . . showed that murders are more prevalent in rural areas*: The 2001 study that found an inverse correlation between murder and population density was Dezhbakhsh, p. 21.

60 *Defenders . . . adhere to the numbers*: For example, Dezhbakhsh, pp. 10–12, accepts the proposition that some homicides are not deterrable, acknowledges there's no verifiable way to categorize which are and which aren't, and claims, nonetheless, those limitations have no impact on his results.

61 *period between conviction and execution . . . eleven and a half years*: U.S. Department of Justice, Bureau of Justice Statistics *Bulletin*, December 2001, p. 1, gave the average time between conviction and execution in 2000 as eleven and a half years.

61 *researchers seem to agree . . . death penalty is more expensive*: A number of cost studies were summarized by the Commission in our Report, pp. 197–99.

61 *new study . . . costs . . . death penalty . . . more*: See Report, p. 198, and M. Goodpaster, "Cost Comparison Between a Death Penalty Case and a Case Where the Charge and Conviction Is Life Without Parole," in Indiana Report, pp. 119–22 F.

62 *amount saved by abolition is small*: See Illinois State Budget Update, Fiscal Year 2003, posted at *http://www.state.il.us/budget/BudSumm 03.pdf*. The Death Penalty Information Center, for example, says: "The most comprehensive study in the country found that the death penalty costs North Carolina $2.16 million per execution *over* the costs of a non–death penalty murder case with a sentence of imprisonment for life" (Duke University, May 1993). The study referred to, "The Costs of Processing Murder Cases in North Carolina," is available on line at *www.pps.aas.duke.edu/people/faculty/ cook/comnc.pdf*. Extrapolating, the DPIC says this means that in the United States we've spent an extra $1 billion since the death penalty was reestablished in 1976. The number is impressive until one bears in mind that it's derived over a period of twenty-seven years. Taking the DPIC estimate as correct nonetheless means that on an average basis, we've spent less than $40 million per year, with the costs spread over the thirty-eight death penalty states. See *http://www.deathpenaltyinfo.org/costs2.html*.

63 *Sometimes a crime is so horrible*: In reapproving capital punishment, the U.S. Supreme Court, in *Gregg v. Georgia*, quoted the following from Lord Justice Denning, Master of the Rolls of the Court of Appeal in England: "Punishment is the way in which society expresses its denunciation of wrong doing: and, in order to maintain respect for law, it is essential that the punishment inflicted for grave crimes should adequately reflect the revulsion felt by the great majority of citizens for them. It is a mistake to consider the objects of

punishment as being deterrent or reformative or preventive and nothing else . . . The truth is that some crimes are so outrageous that society insists on adequate punishment, because the wrongdoer deserves it, irrespective of whether it is a deterrent or not." *Royal Commission on Capital Punishment, Minutes of Evidence*, 12/1/49, p. 207 (1950); 428 U.S. at 184n.30.

64 *can get life . . . for . . . swiping a few videos*: The U.S. Supreme Court allowed to stand the sentence of fifty years to life imposed on Leandro Andrade for stealing videotapes worth a total of $153.54 from two Kmarts. *Lockyer v. Andrade*, _-US – (No. 01-1127, decided 3/5/03).

65 *along with many others*: Memoir, by its nature, is a self-centered form. But I hope my account is clear that Alex's freedom is due to the work of many whose names have otherwise gone unmentioned. At Sonnenschein, we invested thousands of hours in this *pro bono* case, many of them given by Matt Tanner and Leslie Suson, two fine lawyers, and by two heroic paralegals, Mary Kramer and Lynette Johnson. When the appeal was concluded, I inveigled Dan Webb, my former boss as U.S. Attorney and perhaps America's most eminent trial lawyer, into agreeing to represent Alex if he was retried. Webb's shadow—and that of Dane Drobny and David Korupp, who worked with Dan at the firm of Winston and Strawn—was undoubtedly another factor in the prosecutor's decision to ultimately drop the case, as was the acquittal of Rolando Cruz obtained by Tom Breen, Matt Kennelly, Nan Nolan, and the ubiquitous Larry Marshall.

65 *"Why has the state not confessed error"*: See *Victims*, pp. 261–62, for the authors' account of the Hernandez oral argument.

66 *night of October 25, 1994*: Chris Thomas's case was affirmed on appeal, *People v. Thomas*, 178 Ill. 2d 215, 687 N.E.2d 892 (1997). The required version of the facts, from the state's point of view, appears in the opening pages of the opinion. 178 Ill. 2d at 222–29. Further review of the case was denied by the U.S. Supreme Court, 524 U.S. 955 (1998).

66 *Alton Coleman*: For a description of Alton Coleman's crime spree, see J. Greenberg and B. Glauber, "Virginia Charges Two Sniper

Suspects," *Chicago Tribune* [North Sports Final Edition], 11/7/02, Section N, p. 8, including quotations from my friend Jeremy Margolis about the case.

67 *awful, but nonetheless more pedestrian killing*: The cases we regarded as more aggravated than Chris's to which I refer are Sanchez's, described in the opening pages here; *People v. Coleman*, 168 Ill. 2d 509, 660 N.E.2d 919 (1995), regarding the serial murderer; *People v. McNeal*, 175 Ill. 2d 335, 677 N.E.2d 841 (1997), the double murder; *People v. Enis*, 163 Ill. 2d 367, 645 N.E.2d 856 (1994), where the defendant killed his rape victim after she brought charges; *People v. Neal*, 111 Ill. 2d 180, 489 N.E.2d 845 (1985), the beating and stabbing; and *People v. Albanese*, 104 Ill. 2d 504, 473 N.E.2d 1246 (1984), where the defendant killed many family members with arsenic and has since been executed.

67 *death penalty statute . . . in 1977*: See Report, pp. 3–4, for the history of the Illinois Death Penalty statute.

68 *murder of a community policing volunteer a capital offense*: "New Law Aimed at Protecting Community Policing," *Chicago Tribune* [North Sports Final Edition], 7/29/98, p. 3; 720 ILCS 5/9-1(b)(18).

68 *on Illinois' death row . . . thanks to felony-murder*: See Report, pp. 67–75 and p. 78n.14, and Technical Appendix Section 2C, for a thorough analysis of the eligibility factors utilized in Illinois' death row cases.

69 *contract with the Lake County Public Defender's Office*: The Amended Post Conviction Petition we filed for Chris Thomas, with its references to the record assembled, is on line at *http://www.scottturow.com/ ultimatepunishment* [hereafter "Petition"]. Petition at pp. 15–17 describes Chris's lawyers' contract; p. 56, their experience in capital cases.

70 *trial lawyers . . . seemed to regard the case as a clear loser*: See Petition, pp. 56–58, regarding the expectations and activities of Chris's lawyers.

70 *Thomas's aunt . . . had . . . been prosecuted . . . by one of Chris's lawyers*: Petition, pp. 8–13, 57–58, describes dealings between Chris's aunt and the lawyers. In the Petition, we argued that Chris had the wrong lawyers in the eyes of the law and that one or both should have been disqualified because of the prior adverse relationship with a critical defense witness.

70 *aunt distrusted . . . attorneys*: One of Chris's lawyers admitted that the aunt called the lawyer "the devil." See Petition, p. 11.

71 *Illinois Supreme Court has created a Capital Litigation bar*: The Capital Litigation Trust Fund Act is 725 ILCS 124/15 (eff. 1/1/00). Ill. Sup. Ct. Rule 416 sets forth the new requirements for attorneys appearing in capital cases.

71 *Alstory Simon . . . sentenced to thirty-seven years*: Alstory Simon pled guilty in September 1999, but now that he's doing his thirty-seven-year sentence, Simon has claimed that his confession to Porter's investigators was somehow coerced. J. Coen, "Confessed Killer Recants His Story," *Chicago Tribune* [Lake Final Edition], 12/14/02, p. 1. Porter's lawyers have called the claims "ridiculous," but it serves as a case in point for those who wonder why prosecutors generally give the back of their hands to *post-hoc* claims of innocence. They are routine—and routinely unavailing.

71 *other . . . murderers . . . crimes seemed . . . graver*: The other murders that did not result in a death penalty are *People v. Edwards*, 301 Ill. App. 3d 966, 704 N.E.2d 982 (2d Dist. 1998) (four murders); *People v. Matney*, 293 Ill. App. 3d 139, 686 N.E.2d 1239 (2d Dist. 1997) (friend on train tracks); and *People v. Smith*, 241 Ill. App. 3d 446, 608 N.E.2d 1259 (2d Dist. 1993) (mother fed acid to baby). A number of other offenses that we regarded as far worse than Chris's are described at pp. 29–30 of our Answer to the State's Motion to Dismiss Thomas's Post-Conviction Petition, posted on line at *http://www.scottturow.com/ultimatepunishment*.

72 *commissioned Mike Radelet and Glenn Pierce*: The Pierce and Radelet study is part of the Commission Report. See Report, Technical Appendix, Section 1, "Race, Region and Death Sentencing in Illinois 1988–1997," 3/20/02.

72 *race effect*: Section 1, p. 56 (Table 29, Race of Offender). Table 27, p. 55, shows that more than 60 percent of first-degree homicide victims are black and nearly 25 percent are white. According to the 2000 census, 15.6 percent of Illinoisans were black, 75.1 percent white. Section 1, p. 2. In 1987, the U.S. Supreme Court decided *McCleskey v. Kemp*, 481 U.S. 279 (1987), a 5–4 decision that found proven systemic race effects constitutionally insignificant in an individual case. Justice Powell, who wrote the opinion, later told his bi-

ographer it was the worst decision he made on the Court. Jeffries, *Justice Lewis F. Powell, Jr.: A Biography* (Scribner's, 1994), p. 451. The statistical studies at issue in McCleskey showed that in Georgia in the eighties, as in Illinois today, whites charged with capital murder were sentenced to death more often than blacks. 481 U.S. at 286. This is not true in all states, however; see Section 1, Appendix 1, pp. 27–33, for a summary of studies in other states. This suggests that the Illinois numbers may be influenced by geographical disparities, because there are higher rates of death sentencing in largely white areas of the state.

72 *white victim . . . controlling variable*: Section 1, p. 55 (Table 27, Race of Victim). The same table shows the rate at which whites and blacks are condemned for murdering whites. It is also worth noting that the last time the issue was studied in Illinois in 1980, blacks were nearly three times more likely than whites to be death-sentenced for killing a white. See Section 1, pp. 6–8. These days, for statistical purposes the numbers are basically even, with whites given a capital sentence in this circumstance slightly more often. Other states, like Kentucky and Pennsylvania, still condemn black killers of whites more often. Section 1, pp. 29 and 31.

72 *calculation of the harm of a murder*: Indeed, in *Payne v. Tennessee*, 501 U.S. 808 (1991), in which the Supreme Court reauthorized victim impact testimony, the Court recognized that juries may engage in these kinds of comparisons. The Court found that victim impact testimony did not encourage such comparative thinking, but recognized it might occur and appeared to say it is not constitutionally forbidden. *Id*. at 823. ("It is designed to show instead each victim's 'uniqueness as an individual human being,' whatever the jury might think of the loss to the community resulting from his death might be.")

73 *murders are gang-related*: D. Heinzmann, "Chicago Falls Out of 1st in Murders," *Chicago Tribune* [Final C edition], 1/1/03, p. 1, shows that Chicago has the nation's highest murder rate, as it has had for eight of the last nine years, and that police attribute roughly half of Chicago murders to gangs and/or drugs. See also "Chicago, Big-City Murder Capital," *Chicago Tribune* [North Sports Final edition], 1/16/03, Section 1, p. 18.

73 *Geography . . . matters in Illinois*: Section 1, p. 18, discusses geographical data for Illinois.

73 *Capital punishment for slaying a woman*: Gender-related statistics are discussed at Section 1, p. 18. Note that because of the small sample, the prevalence of death sentences for men compared to women is not statistically significant, according to the authors.

74 *justices . . . have debated*: Justices Blackmun and Scalia, for example, went back and forth on the constitutional effect of individualized decision-making in *Callins v. James*, 510 U.S. 1141 (1994), the decision where Justice Blackmun issued his famous dissent containing his promise to tinker no further with the machinery of death.

76 *Court ruled against Chris*: *People v. Thomas*, 178 Ill. 2d 215, 687, N.E.2d 892 (1997), *cert. denied*, 524 U.S. 955 (1998).

77 *unfathomably complex*: Writers sometimes make mistakes, and I may make more than my share. Readers are good about correcting the errors they find. For example, many readers wrote to me about my novel *Reversible Errors*, discussed below, to point out that the murder weapon, a Smith and Wesson .38 five-shot Chief's Special, does not have a safety, as the first edition of the book had asserted. When an early version of part of this book appeared in *The New Yorker*, two lawyers, including the estimable Laurence Tribe of Harvard, wrote to question my discussion of the Supreme Court's decision in *Witherspoon v. Illinois*. But although I've had much correspondence from death penalty experts about *Reversible Errors*, none of them has raised any question about the framework I posited for resolution of Rommy Gandolph's last-ditch death penalty appeal, even though those procedures are entirely invented. (For the buffs: I imagined that on a second *habeas corpus* petition, the appellate court had ordered the district court to grant discovery on appealability.) That is because, frankly, the law is such a thicket in this area that I doubt anybody's sure whether I'm right or wrong. Personally, I thought the hearings I imagined were possible under the law. But I found no precedent.

77 *Judge Barbara Gilleran Johnson . . . ruled*: Judge Gilleran Johnson's order [hereafter "Order"] is posted at *http://www.scottturow.com/ultimatepunishment*. See Order at 3–4. It came on the state's motion to dismiss our Petition. Because the facts in the case were not dis-

puted, her decision on the legal issues was effectively a ruling on the merits, and both parties had asserted as much to the Court when the case was argued.

78 *Illinois Supreme Court ... finding ... which was flatly untrue*: See *People v. Thomas*, 178 Ill. 2d at 247, 687 N.E.2d at 906. See Order at 3.

79 *more extensive picture of Thomas's background*: Petition, pp. 60–67, sets forth the evidence we gathered about Chris's background. The Order at 5 found that it would have been "better practice" for this information to have been presented at Chris's sentencing, but did not reach the issue of whether it was ineffective assistance of counsel, in light of the prior ruling on misuse of Chris's mental health records.

79 *"Yes, I would," he answered*: Chris was resentenced on December 15, 1999. He made the remarks quoted at pp. 30–32 of the transcript, which is posted at *http://www.scottturow.com/ultimatepunishment*.

80 *Coleman spent seventeen years ... without ... disciplinary write-up*: The *Dayton Daily News* of 4/27/02 contained the quote about Coleman. The lawyer for Coleman to whom I refer is Dale Baich, Office of the Federal Public Defender, 222 North Central Avenue, Suite 810, Phoenix, Arizona 85004.

83 *"I-57 murderer"*: Details of the I-57 killings and of Brisbon's apprehension for the crime are set forth in *People v. Brisbon*, 89 Ill. App. 3d 513, 411 N.E.2d 956 (1st Dist. 1980).

83 *after the sentencing, Brisbon*: Details of Brisbon's second murder conviction and of his two sentencing hearings (the first was reversed) are set forth at *People v. Brisbon*, 106 Ill. 2d 342, 478 N.E.2d 402, 88 Ill. Dec. 8 (1985) (where the prosecutor's remark about the relative length of Brisbon's sentence is repeated), and *People v. Brisbon*, 129 Ill. 2d 200, 544 N.E.2d 297, 135 Ill. Dec. 801 (1989). Brisbon's disciplinary record at the time of his death sentence is discussed in those opinions and *People v. Brisbon*, 164 Ill. 2d 236, 647 N.E.2d 935, 207 Ill. Dec. 442 (1995).

84 *continued to compile ... disciplinary dossier*: Information regarding Brisbon's discipline since 1982 provided through the Illinois Department of Corrections.

84 *Tamms Correctional Center*: Information about Tamms is posted at the Illinois Department of Corrections Web site, *http://www.idoc .state.il.us/subsections/facilities/information.asp?instchoice=tam*, and in a

brochure available at the institution, 200 E. Supermax Road, P.O. Box 400, Tamms, IL 62988; (618) 747–2042.

84 *clearly prone to murder again*: The number of murderers destined to repeat their crimes actually appears relatively small. For example, in a nationwide study published in 1989 of 558 prisoners who'd had their death sentences commuted by *Furman*, seven murders had been committed by five persons; six murders occurred in the penitentiary, and one after release. J. Marquart and J. Sorensen, "A National Study of *Furman*-Commuted Prisoners: Assessing the Threat to Society from Capital Offenders," reprinted in *The Death Penalty in America*, p. 162; see also H. Bedau, "Prison Homicide, Recidivist Murder and Life Sentences," in *The Death Penalty in America*, p. 176. The authors thought their data called into question the notion that the future dangerousness of murderers in general justified the death penalty.

86 *objections from the left*: See, for example, R. Good, "The Super-Max Solution," *The Nation*, 3/3/03, p. 7, describing a lawsuit filed on behalf of four mentally ill Tamms inmates, claiming that the enforced isolation of the facility fosters mental instability.

86 *Tamms is expensive*: Cost figures are from the Illinois Department of Corrections. The cost of confinement at Tamms is placed at more than $52,000 per prisoner on the facility's Web site, *http://www .idoc.state.il.us/subsections/facilities/information.asp?instchoice=tam*. The same figure is a little over $22,000 at the state's largest and most notorious prison, the Stateville facility near Joliet. *http://www.idoc .state.il.us/subsections/facilities/information.asp?instchoice=sta*.

89 *we had reached a broad consensus*: The Preamble to the Report, p. i., set forth the Commission's points of general agreement.

90 *a series of rule changes . . . by the Illinois Supreme Court*: In addition to establishing a Capital Litigation Bar, new Illinois Supreme Court Rule 416 requires prosecutors to make up their minds about whether they're going to pursue the death penalty within 120 days of arraignment, ending the prior practice under which defense lawyers in many first-degree murder cases never knew before trial if they had to prepare for a death penalty hearing. The Court also requires case management conferences in capital cases, and certifications from both sides. Defense lawyers must certify that they've

fully advised their client about the case, and prosecutors that they've met with investigators and have turned over all discoverable material to the defense. New Rule 417 establishes a protocol for admission of DNA evidence.

90 *wrong cases had reached death row*: For example, at the time *Furman* was decided, Illinois had only 31 persons on death row, as opposed to the 171 who were there at the end of 2002. See J. Marquart and J. Sorensen, "A National Study of *Furman*-Commuted Prisoners: Assessing the Threat to Society from Capital Offenders," reprinted in *The Death Penalty in America*, p. 164.

90 *all . . . interrogations . . . videotaped*: See Report, Recommendations 4–7, pp. 24–28, for the discussion of videotaping and related proposals. See also p. 33, discussing related jury instructions.

90 *altering lineup procedures*: The Recommendations regarding identification procedures are numbers 10–15, Report, pp. 31–40.

90 *pretrial hearings to determine the reliability of . . . informants*: Recommendations 51 and 52, Report, pp. 121–23, set forth proposed procedures regarding in-custody informants.

90 *death sentence not . . . imposed without . . . concurrence . . . trial judge*: Trial judge concurrence in death sentences was outlined in Recommendation 66, Report, pp. 152–54.

90 *banning . . . death penalty . . . based solely on . . . lone eyewitness or . . . accomplice*: Recommendation 69, Report, p. 158, would bar capital sentences when based on the uncorroborated testimony of a single eyewitness or jailed informant.

91 *eligibility criteria . . . trimmed to five*: Our proposals for reduced eligibility criteria, Recommendations 27 and 28, were set forth and explained at Report, pp. 65–79.

91 *urged creation of a statewide oversight body*: Recommendation 30, Report, pp. 84–88, details the composition and function of the proposed statewide review panel.

91 *guaranteed sentences of natural life*: Recommendation 67, Report, pp. 155–56, proposed the new mandatory natural life sentence for death-eligible cases.

91 *expediting . . . post-conviction*: Recommendations 72–75, Report, pp. 169–176, set forth our ideas for trying to shorten the death penalty endgame.

91 *major newspapers endorsed . . . as did . . . state bar*: The State Bar Association endorsed seventy-six of our eighty-five proposals, including the state review commission and reducing death penalty eligibility. See *ISBA Bar News*, vol. 43, no. 1, 7/15/02, *http://www.isba.org/ association/027%2D15a.htm*.

91 *state prosecutors' organization . . . dug in its heels*: The state prosecutors' association responded on May 16, 2002, with its own report. See Illinois State's Attorneys Association, Response to the Report of the Governor Ryan's Commission on Capital Punishment, 5/16/02, and "Ryan Panel Plans Hit by Prosecutors," *Chicago Tribune*, 5/17/02.

92 *major players . . . supported significant changes*: Response to the Commission report in its aftermath and in the months following was regularly documented in the local press. S. Mills and C. Parsons, "Ryan's Panel Urges Fixes in Death Penalty; 2-Year Study Says Fatal Flaw Exists," *Chicago Tribune* [Sports Final, CN Edition], 4/15/02, p. 1; "Justice Demands Death Penalty Fix," Chicagoland *Daily Herald*, 4/17/02; S. Mills and M. Possley, " 'We're Talking About Life and Death . . . Not About Losing an Election,' Reform Plan Would Have Kept 115 from a Cell on Death Row," *Chicago Tribune* [North Sports Final Edition], 4/16/02, p. 1; "Nothing Short of Justice," *Chicago Tribune* [North Sports Final Edition], 4/16/02, p. 18; M. Possley and E. Ferkenhoff, "Daley, Cops Question Death Penalty Reform Plan," *Chicago Tribune* [North Sports Final Edition], 4/17/02, p. 1; R. Pearson, "Governor Hopefuls Differ on Death-Eligible Crimes, Ryan Sees It Only For 'Worst of Worst,' " *Chicago Tribune* [McHenry County, MC Edition], 4/23/02; R. Pearson, "Candidates Agree on Reform; Birkett, Madigan Say Death Penalty Plan Goes Too Far," *Chicago Tribune*, 4/26/02; "Fixing the Death Penalty Series: Restoring Justice. First of five parts," *Chicago Tribune* [Chicagoland Final Edition], 9/29/02, p. 10. (The remaining four parts of the series appeared on successive days.)

92 *none . . . enacted*: C. Parsons and R. Long, "Death Penalty Reform Falters; House Rejects Ryan Plan As Senate Works on Compromise," *Chicago Tribune* [Lake Final Edition], 11/20/02, p. 1.

92 *"headed straight for the trash bin"*: Senator Dillard was quoted in

S. Mills and C. Parsons, "Ryan's Panel Urges Fixes in Death Penalty; 2-Year Study Says Fatal Flaw Exists," *Chicago Tribune* [Sports Final, CN Edition], 4/15/02, p. 1. His role in sponsoring legislation embodying the commission's reforms is described in J. Patterson, "Ryan Urges Legislators to Hurry, Approve Death Penalty Reforms," Chicagoland *Daily Herald*, 5/14/02; C. Parsons, "Ryan Making End Run on Death Penalty; Veto Could Set Up Vote in Legislature," *Chicago Tribune* [North Final Edition], 8/24/02, p. 1.

92 *June, I testified*: I testified before the Illinois State Senate Capital Litigation Subcommittee on June 26, 2002.

93 *General Assembly . . . added a twenty-first factor*: Public Act 92-0854. See *http://www.law.northwestern.edu/faculty/fulltime/bienen/bienen.html, Seminar Task Force Report: Murder and Its Consequences*, p. 94.

93 *lawyers . . . petition the Governor to exercise . . . clemency*: See S. Mills, "Clemency Push for All 160 on Death Row," *Chicago Tribune*, 5/16/02.

93 *victims and prosecutors appeared . . . before the Prisoner Review Board*: See J. Keilman, "Clemency Pleas Rile Panelists; Some Attack Defense Claims, Hearings' Pace," *Chicago Tribune* [Northwest Final, NW Edition], 10/17/02, p. 1; S. Mills and C. Parsons, "Tears Send a Message; Hearings' Emotional Impact Surprises Death Penalty Foes," *Chicago Tribune* [Chicagoland Final Edition], 10/27/02, p. 1; H. G. Meyer, "Death Penalty Foes Rally Near Hearings," *Chicago Tribune* [North Final Edition], 10/26/02, p. 17; J. Keilman and S. Kapos, "Attack Victims Speak at Hearings; Survivors Recall Horrors, Seek to Influence Ryan," *Chicago Tribune* [North Sports Final Edition], 10/24/02, p. 1; S. Mills, "Life-or-Death Debate Rages at Hearings; Attorneys Argue over Clemency As Victims' Families Relive Grief, Pain," *Chicago Tribune* [North Sports Final Edition], 10/16/02, p. 1; E. Zorn, "Prosecutors Are Directors in Theater of Pain," *Chicago Tribune* [North Sports Final Edition], 10/24/02, p. 1.

93 *Death penalty opponents responded with . . . mediagenic events*: C. Jones, " 'Exonerated' an Enlightening Evening for Ryan," *Chicago Tribune* [North Sports Final, C Edition], 12/18/02, p. 1; D. Mendell, "March from Death Row; Ex-Inmates Carry Plea to Governor

from Stateville," *Chicago Tribune* [North Sports Final Edition], 12/17/02, p. 1; W. Hageman, "2 Days of Events on Wrongful Convictions," *Chicago Tribune* [Chicagoland Final Edition], 12/15/02, p. 3.

94 *Governor might have had some role in unsavory doings*: M. O'Connor and R. Gibson, "U.S. Links Ryan to Cover-up; Prosecutors Say He Knew Campaign Records Would Be Destroyed," *Chicago Tribune* [North Sports Final Edition], 12/19/02, p. 1.

94 *Ryan . . . vetoed bills that . . . added new eligibility factors*: See Report, p. 16, nn. 13–14, for a full discussion of the new death penalty provisions Governor Ryan vetoed.

94 *firsthand experience . . . prosecutorial power*: I do not intend any criticism of the prosecutors who investigated George Ryan. After obtaining more than fifty convictions related to the Secretary of State's office under Ryan, they more than justified their inquiries.

96 *Ryan pardoned four men on death row*: The four men pardoned were Stanley Howard, Madison Hobley, Leroy Orange, and Aaron Patterson. S. Mills and C. Parsons, " 'The System Has Failed'; Ryan Condemns Injustice, Pardons 6; Paves the Way for Sweeping Clemency," *Chicago Tribune* [North Final Edition], 1/11/03, p. 19. See also *People v. Stanley Howard*, 147 Ill. 2d 103, 588 N.E.2d 1044 (1992); *People v. Madison Hobley*, 159 Ill. 2d 272, 637 N.E.2d 992 (1994); 182 Ill. 2d 404, 696 N.E.2d 313 (1998); *People v. Leroy Orange*, 121 Ill. 2d 364, 521 N.E.2d 69 (1988); 168 Ill. 2d 138, 659 N.E.2d 935 (1995); 195 Ill. 2d 437, 749 N.E.2d 932 (2001); *People v. Aaron Patterson*, 154 Ill. 2d 414, 610 N.E.2d 16 (1992); 192 Ill.2d 93, 735 N.E. 2d 616 (2000). See also R. Bush and J. Coen, "3 Awaken to Busy Day of Freedom," *Chicago Tribune* [Chicagoland Final Edition], 1/12/03, p. 14; "Excerpts from Ryan Speech at DePaul," *Chicago Tribune* [Chicagoland Edition], 1/12/03, p. 16; "Freed from Death Row," *Chicago Tribune* [Chicagoland Edition], 1/12/03, p. 8; "Excerpts from Gov. Ryan's Speech," *Chicago Tribune* [North Final Edition], 1/11/03, p. 18.

96 *evidence . . . found to show . . . torture*: Burge's alleged torture, and the investigation of it, are well described in J. Conroy, "A Hell of a Deal," *Chicago Reader*, 10/12/01, posted at *http://www.todesstrafe-usa.de/death_penalty/alive_patterson.htm*. In a 1997 opinion, U.S.

District Court Judge Milton Shadur wrote: "It is now common knowledge that in the early to mid-1980s Chicago Police Commander Jon Burge and many officers working under him regularly engaged in the physical abuse and torture of prisoners to extract confessions . . . Both internal police accounts and numerous lawsuits and appeals brought by suspects alleging such abuse substantiate that those beatings and other means of torture occurred as an established practice, not just on an isolated basis." *United States ex rel. Maxwell v. Gilmore*, 37 F. Supp. 2d 1078, 1094 (N.D.Ill. 1999). See also *People v. Wilson*, 116 Ill. 2d 29, 506 N.E.2d 571, 106 Ill. Dec. 771 (1987), finding that convicted cop killer Andrew Wilson had been beaten into confessing, which culminated in a successful civil rights suit against the city of Chicago. See *Wilson v. City of Chicago*, 120 F.3d 681 (7th Cir. 1997); R. Kaiser, "Burge a Distant Memory at Far South Side Station; Ex-Cop Brass' Abuse Cited by Ryan in Pardons," *Chicago Tribune* [Chicagoland Edition], 1/12/03, p. 14. The Cook County State's Attorney's Office had long opposed the efforts of these four defendants—and several others—to gain post-trial evidentiary hearings into the torture charges, even after their claims had gained substance from the revelations in other cases. In the meantime, nearly a decade after the evidence of torture had emerged, no criminal charges had been brought against any officer. The Chief Judge of the Circuit Court of Cook County ruled in 2002 that the State's Attorney's Office had a conflict of interest and appointed a special prosecutor to conduct a criminal investigation of Area Two officers. S. Mills and J. Hanna, "Counsel to Probe Torture by Police," *Chicago Tribune* [North Sports Final Edition], 4/25/02, p. 1.

96 *In . . . four pardoned cases . . . principal evidence . . . was a confession*: Madison Hobley, one of the four men who was pardoned, has long contended that he was tortured but never actually gave the oral confession that was used to convict him of setting a fire that killed seven people, including his wife and infant son. See *People v. Hobley*, 182 Ill. 2d 404, 696 N.E.2d 313 (1998), where Hobley was granted an evidentiary hearing to show that the state had suppressed evidence. The Illinois Supreme Court said Hobley's "petition make[s] a substantial showing that the State has acted with bad faith in sup-

pressing exculpatory evidence throughout the course of proceedings in defendant's case."

96 *Aaron Patterson*: For a comprehensive account of Patterson's case, see J. Conroy, "Pure Torture," *Chicago Reader*, 12/3/99, *http://www.ccadp.org/aaronpatterson-reader.htm*. The Illinois Supreme Court had decided that Patterson was entitled to an evidentiary hearing on his torture claim because the trial judge who had rejected those contentions had refused to consider Patterson's written message about what was happening to him, incorrectly deeming it inadmissible hearsay. *People v. Patterson*, 192 Ill. 2d 93, 735 N.E.2d 616 (2000).

97 *only eyewitnesses who'd seen Brisbon . . . recanted*: See Remarks Concerning Clemency Petition of Henry Brisbon Presented to the Illinois Prisoner Review Board, 10/15/02 (presentation of Brisbon's lawyer, Jean MacLean Snyder of the MacArthur Justice Center) Link at *http://macarthur.uchicago.edu/deathpenalty/brisbon.html*; *United States ex rel. Brisbon v. Gilmore* (U.S.D.C.N.D.Ill. No. 95 C 5033 6/5/97) 1997 U.S. Dist. LEXIS 8314.

97 *Kenneth Allen*: See *People v. Allen*, 79 Ill. 2d 471, 405 N.E. 2d 747 (1980) (Remand on Supreme Court's Order to Examine Plea); 101 Ill. 2d 24, 461 N.E.2d 337 (1984); "Death Row Inmates Receive Life," *Chicago Tribune* [Chicagoland Final Edition], 1/12/03, Section 1, p. 18 [hereafter "*Tribune* Case Capsules"].

98 *Latasha Pulliam*: *People v. Pulliam*, 176 Ill. 2d 261, 680 N.E.2d 343 (1997); *People v. Pulliam*, No. 89141 (Ill. Supreme Ct., decided 10/18/02) (remanding for hearing on retardation); *Tribune* Case Capsules, p. 19.

98 *Andrew Johnson*: *People v. Andrew Johnson*, 149 Ill. 2d 118, 594 N.E.2d 253 (1992); 183 Ill. 2d 176, 700 N.E.2d 996 (1998), *Tribune* Case Capsules, p. 18.

98 *Ryan commuted the sentences of the 167 persons left on death row*: M. Possley and S. Mills, "Clemency for All; Ryan Commutes 164 Death Sentences to Life in Prison Without Parole; 'There Is No Honorable Way to Kill,' He Says," *Chicago Tribune* [Chicagoland Final Edition], 1/12/03, p. 1; S. Mills, "After Years of Soul Searching, Ryan Decides Not to 'Play God,' " *Chicago Tribune* [Chicagoland Final Edition], 1/12/03, p. 1.

99 *Justice Blackmun wrote, in a famous dissent*: Callins v. James, 510 U.S. 1141, 1143 (1994).

99 *A number of prosecutors, police officers, and survivors expressed outrage*: M. Possley and S. Mills, "Clemency for All; Ryan Commutes 164 Death Sentences to Life in Prison Without Parole; 'There Is No Honorable Way to Kill,' He Says," *Chicago Tribune* [Chicagoland Final Edition], 1/12/03, p. 15; J. Kellman, "Relatives of Victims Feel Cheated," *Chicago Tribune* [Chicagoland Final Edition], 1/12/03, p. 1.

99 *The* St. Louis Post-Dispatch . . . *published poll results*: "Illinoisans Are Split Closely on Ryan's Commutations," *St. Louis Post-Dispatch*, 2/7/03. The poll showed that 50.5 percent of respondents disagreed with Ryan and 47.5 percent agreed, bringing the results within the poll's margin of error. Intriguingly, the response in Illinois closely mirrored reactions in the rest of the country. In a national poll, conducted by Harris Interactive for CNN and *Time*, those with opinions were evenly divided about whether Governor Ryan had done the right thing. Harris Interactive, 1/17/03. See *http://www.deathpenaltyinfo.org/Polls.html#ABCNewsWashPost12403*.

100 *a bill to abolish . . . received a favorable vote*: H.B. 213. See *http://www.legis.state.il.us/legislation/default.asp*; K. McCann and C. Parsons, "Death Penalty Debate Gets Forum in House," *Chicago Tribune* [Chicago Final Edition], 3/7/03, p. 1; "House Panel: End Death Penalty," *Chicago Tribune* [RedEye Edition] 3/7/03, p. 6.

100 *One bill mandated videotaping interrogations*: For further details see *http://www.legis.state.il.us/legislation/default.asp*, and C. Parsons and K. McCann, "Taped Confessions Bill Passes; Governor Says He Will Sign Measure Requiring Record in Homicide Interrogations," *Chicago Tribune*, [Chicago Final Edition], 5/9/03, p. 1. For some history of the legislation, see "A Remarkable Week for Justice," *Chicago Tribune*, 4/7/03 (Editorial) and C. Parsons and K. McCann, "Senate OKs Death-Penalty Bills," *Chicago Tribune*, 4/4/03 (Metro Section).

100 *A second . . . reform measure . . . passed . . . in late May*: SB 472, viewable at *http://www.legis.state.il.us/legislation*. See also C. Parsons and R. Long, "Death Penalty Reform Goes to Blagojevich," *Chicago Tribune* [Chicago Final Edition], 5/30/03, p. 1.

101 *the new Governor . . . promised to sign the videotaping bill*: C. Parsons and K. McCann, "Taped Confessions Bill Passes; Governor Says He Will Sign Measure Requiring Record in Homicide Interrogations," *Chicago Tribune* [Chicago Final Edition], 5/9/03, p. 1. See also T. Sullivan and S. Turow, "Taping Interrogations a Much-Needed Reform," *Chicago Tribune* [Chicago Final Edition], 5/6/03, p. 23.

101 *Blagojevich also spoke favorably about the broader reform*: New reports on May 29 and 30 describe the new Governor's remarks about the reform bill and his comments about lifting the moratorium, and details of the legislative action. C. Parsons and R. Long, "Death Penalty Reform Goes to Blagojevich," *Chicago Tribune* [Chicago Final Edition], 5/30/03, p. 1; S. McLaughlin, "House Advances Death Penalty Reform," *Kankakee Daily Journal*, Metro Section, 5/30/03; "Senate Sends Sweeping Death Penalty Reform to Governor," at *http://abclocal.go.com/wls/news/052903_ns_deathpenalty.html*.

105 *Arthur's reflections about the world of criminal law*: *Reversible Errors* (Farrar, Straus and Giroux, 2002), pp. 6–7.

111 *jailers . . . find an execution . . . unsettling*: *Witness to an Execution*, by Sound Portraits Productions (2000), an audio record of the reflections of Jim Willett, former Warden at the death house in Huntsville, Texas, as well as of other correctional personnel, shows how discomforting an execution is for those who perform it. See *www.soundportraits.org*.

111 *Easley . . . evidence at his sentencing hearing*: *People v. Ike J. Easley, Jr.*, 148 Ill. 2d 281, 346, 592 N.E.2d 1036, 1065, 170 Ill. Dec. 356 (1992).

113 *conservatives with growing doubts*: For a survey of many opinions about capital punishment, including conservative critics of the death penalty, see, for example, W. Saletan's article, "Calculating the Risk," in July/August 2000 issue of *Mother Jones*, posted at *http://www.motherjones.com/mother_jones/JA00/power_ja00.html*. George Will, probably the nation's most highly regarded conservative columnist, has expressed continuing reservations about capital punishment. Notwithstanding those, however, he excoriated Governor's Ryan's blanket commutations in his syndicated column, "Unhealable Wounds," *The Washington Post*, 1/19/03, p. B7. Will repeated a comment he had made before—"Conservatives, especially, should remember that capital punishment is a government program, so

skepticism is warranted"—and also observed, "By causing courts to multiply restrictions on the imposition of capital punishment, opponents of such punishment have helped make its administration capricious, thereby doubling the arguments against it: capriciousness, and the fact that this reduces the death penalty's ability to deter, and even the ability of social science to measure its deterrent power." Will found the best argument for capital punishment the one I've dubbed "moral proportion." In support, he quoted—me, a passage from *Reversible Errors*. His column is posted at *http://www.jewishworldreview.com/cols/will012103.asp*.

115 *the Menendez brothers . . . or the Unabomber*: For a comprehensive description of the crimes of Erik and Lyle Menendez, see *http://www.crimelibrary.com/menendez/menendezmain.htm*. A lengthy résumé of the Unabomber investigation and the legal proceedings leading to life imprisonment for Theodore Kaczynski is on the Web at *http://www.cnn.com/SPECIALS/1997/unabomb/*.

115 *justices . . . have waffled*: Compare Blackmun's dissent in *Callins v. James*, 510 U.S. 1141, 1143 (1994), with his dissent in *Furman v. Georgia*, 408 U.S. at 407–9. Compare Justice Powell's dissent in *Furman*, 408 U.S. at 421–27, his opinion in *Gregg v. Georgia*, 428 U.S. 153 (1976), and his opinion in *McKleskey v. Kemp*, 481 U.S. 279 (1987), with his comments to his biographer about *McKleskey*. Jeffries, *Justice Lewis F. Powell, Jr: A Biography* (1994), p. 451. Compare Justice Stevens's opinion in *Gregg* with his dissent in *McKleskey*, 481 U.S. at 368, where he stated that the Constitution will not tolerate a racially discriminatory death penalty, and suggested that the Georgia statute he had approved in *Gregg* be dramatically narrowed. Compare Justice White's concurring opinion in *Furman*, 408 U.S. at 311–14, with his concurrence in *Gregg*, 428 U.S. at 207, and Justice Stewart's concurrence in *Furman*, 408 U.S. at 306–11, with his opinion in *Gregg*.

# ACKNOWLEDGMENTS

A number of persons are due special thanks for their help in the writing of this book. Beyond my fellow members of the Illinois Capital Punishment Commission, the staff that supported us under Matt Bettenhausen's guidance was remarkably professional and informed. To the estimable Jean Templeton and to Nancy Miller, both of whom continued to answer my questions and provide assistance long after the Commission's work was complete, I owe deep and prolonged bows of gratitude, as I also do to Rick Guzman.

Aside from the Commission staff, Rachel Turow offered extensive and unerring research assistance over a number of months, which was essential to my work. My thanks, too, to Chris Thomas for letting me discuss our communications in instances where I would not have done so without his permission.

I am also grateful to a number of persons at *The New*

*Yorker* for their help with the article on which part of this book is based: David Remnick for commissioning it, Jeff Toobin for encouraging me, Marina Harss and Nandi Rodrigo for scrupulous fact-checking, and Sharon Delano for a number of useful editorial suggestions. To my editor and publisher at Farrar Straus, Jonathan Galassi, who has long urged me to write extended nonfiction about the law, my debt of gratitude only grows deeper.

My partners at Sonnenschein Nath & Rosenthal, and in particular our Chair, my dear friend Duane Quaini, who have long supported the legal work that much of this book describes are also due my thanks. Mary Kramer, the superb paralegal who not only organized, but also frequently appeared to have memorized, the vast legal record in both the Hernandez and Thomas cases, once again provided unhesitating aid while I was writing. Without my secretary at SNR, Ellie Lucas, and my personal administrative aide, Kathy Conway, who wrestled the end notes into submission, there is no telling what might have happened.

As always, no thanks are adequate for Annette for her consistent insight and encouragement.

Any mistakes that remain, despite the dogged efforts of all of these persons, are only my fault.